HEART HEALTHY COOKBOOK FOR BEGINNERS

2000+ Days Of Simple And Tasty Recipes For A Strong Heart: Lower Your Blood Pressure And Reduce Cholesterol With Low-Fat And Low-Sodium Dishes

Susan McKnight

COPYRIGHT

TABLE OF CONTENTS

Chapter 9
Breakfast

Chapter 10
Lunch

Chapter 11

Snacks

Chapter 12

Beverages

Chapter 13

Dinner

Chapter 14
Desserts

Bonus 1
28-Day Meal Plan

Bonus 2
Shopping List

BONUS 3
FAQs Regarding The 28-Day Meal Plan

INTRODUCTION

Did you know that nearly half of all adults in the United States have some form of cardiovascular disease? It's a startling reality that underscores the critical importance of heart health and the undeniable influence our diets have on it. Across the globe, heart disease does not discriminate, affecting people from all walks of life, driven significantly by our lifestyle choices, particularly what we eat. Our daily dietary decisions can be our most powerful ally in combating heart disease, shaping our overall health and longevity.

This book, packed with 90 carefully curated recipes, is designed to be your guide in the culinary journey towards a heart-healthy lifestyle. It's not merely a cookbook but a comprehensive guide to rethinking how we nourish our bodies for optimal heart health. From antioxidant-rich smoothies to start your day, to protein-packed dinners that satisfy without compromising your well-being, each recipe is a step towards transforming your health, one delicious meal at a time.

But this book aims to do more than just educate you on heart-healthy eating. It's here to inspire a profound and lasting change in your eating habits and to offer practical, tasty solutions for incorporating heart-friendly foods into every meal. Despite the grim statistics, there is a beacon of hope. Positive changes are within reach for anyone, regardless of their starting point. Small, consistent adjustments in our diet can lead to significant improvements in heart health.

What sets this book apart is its foundation in simplicity and scientific evidence. We demystify the complexities of heart health, translating cutting-edge research into practical steps you can take to protect your heart. This isn't about overhauling your diet overnight but about making manageable, enjoyable changes that fit into your lifestyle for the long haul.

My motivation for writing this book stems from a personal journey marked by loss and a deep-seated desire to prevent others from experiencing similar heartache. It's a culmination of personal experiences, rigorous research, and a genuine wish to make a meaningful impact. This book is more than a collection of recipes; it's a mission to empower you with the knowledge and tools needed to live a heart-healthy life.

As we embark on this journey together, you'll navigate through chapters that not only introduce you to heart-friendly foods but also teach you how to balance nutrients effectively, adapt your favorite recipes for better heart health, and implement practical strategies for a lifestyle conducive to cardiovascular wellness.

I invite you now to turn the page with an open heart and mind, ready to embrace the transformative power of nutrition. Let this book serve as your first step towards a healthier heart and a more vibrant life. The path to heart health starts with a single, informed choice. Are you ready to take that step?

CHAPTER 1
HEART HEALTH

Every year, millions of people face heart health challenges, but a single step can steer us towards a healthier heart. This chapter opens the door to a clearer understanding of your heart's health and the risks that lurk around the corner. It's not just about avoiding problems; it's about building a strong foundation for a life filled with energy and joy. Let's dive into the heart of what keeps us ticking and learn how to keep it beating strong.

The heart, a fist-sized powerhouse, pumps life through our body every second of every day without rest. Its job? To send oxygen-rich blood to every part of our body, keeping us alive and kicking. But what keeps the heart happy? The answer lies in the balance of a healthy diet, regular physical activity, and managing stress. Think of your heart as the most diligent worker who thrives on the right fuel and a good work environment. Give it greasy, unhealthy foods, and a couch-potato lifestyle, and it struggles. Feed it nutritious meals and a dose of daily movement, and it flourishes. It's simple: a happy heart means a happier you.

But here's where it gets tricky. Our lives are dotted with unseen risks that can throw a wrench in the works. High blood pressure, sky-high cholesterol levels, and a lifestyle that has us glued to our seats are the main culprits behind heart disease. Each one can sneak up quietly, making it essential to know what to watch out for. High blood pressure acts like a silent enemy, causing the heart to work overtime and wear out. Cholesterol is a bit like a bad roommate for your blood vessels, leaving unwanted clutter that blocks the flow of blood. And sitting all day? It's as harmful as a diet of only junk food. These risks sound daunting, but the good news is, with a few adjustments, they're manageable. It's all about taking those first steps towards a healthier routine, choosing better meals, and shaking off the sedentary dust with some good old-fashioned exercise.

Understanding our heart's needs and the dangers it faces is the first step in a journey toward lasting health. This chapter isn't just about scaring you into action; it's about arming you with the knowledge to make smart, heart-healthy choices every day. With each page, we'll unravel how to turn these risks around and pave the way for a strong, happy heart.

Fundamentals of Cardiovascular Health

Unlocking the secrets of heart health is simpler than decoding an ancient mystery. At its core, our heart is the engine that powers our very existence, beating around 100,000 times a day to send life-giving blood to every corner of our body. This relentless rhythm sustains us, fuels us, and asks for only one thing in return: care.

Caring for this tireless engine means tuning into the essentials of cardiovascular health. The quality of fuel we provide our body, the level of activity we engage in, and how we manage the storms of stress play starring roles in this epic of heart health.

Diet: Your Heart's Fuel

Imagine your heart as a car. Just as a car runs smoothly on the right type of fuel, so does your heart. Foods rich in nutrients, fibers, and healthy fats are premium fuel. They keep the engine running efficiently, without the gunk of unhealthy fats and sugars clogging the system. Incorporating a rainbow of fruits, vegetables, lean proteins, and whole grains into your diet isn't just a feast for the eyes; it's the top-tier maintenance plan your heart needs to thrive.

Exercise: The Heart's Gym

Now, think of exercise as the heart's personal gym session. Just like muscles grow stronger with use, your heart benefits immensely from regular physical activity. A brisk walk, a dance session in your living room, or a cycle through the park isn't just fun; it's your heart's way of lifting weights. This kind of movement keeps the heart's arteries flexible and blood flowing smoothly, reducing the risk of heart-related issues down the line.

Stress Management: The Heart's Meditation

Lastly, consider stress the rust that can erode your heart's health if left unchecked. In today's whirlwind of life, stress is as common as the air we breathe, but managing it is crucial for cardiovascular health. Techniques like deep breathing, mindfulness, and finding hobbies that relax you are akin to giving your heart a peaceful retreat. They lower blood pressure and ensure your heart isn't overworking itself in the face of life's challenges.

Risk Factors for Cardiovascular Diseases

In a world where our health often takes the backseat, it's crucial to spotlight the silent threats that quietly undermine our heart's well-being. Hypertension, high cholesterol, and a sedentary lifestyle are not just buzzwords—they are real risks that can lead to serious heart issues if left unchecked. Understanding these risks is like learning to read a map in unfamiliar territory; it equips you to navigate towards safety.

Hypertension: The Silent Strain

Imagine your blood vessels as highways and your blood as the vehicles on them. Now, picture traffic moving at a safe, steady pace—that's your heart under normal conditions. Hypertension occurs when this traffic speeds up unnaturally, putting pressure on the highway walls (your blood vessels). Over time, this constant pressure can lead to wear and tear, much like a road becomes potholed and damaged with too much heavy traffic. The scary part? Hypertension often whispers so softly that you might not hear it until it's too late. The key to steering clear of this silent strain lies in regular check-ups and simple lifestyle changes like cutting down on salt and practicing relaxation techniques.

High Cholesterol: The Clogged Pathways

Now, envision your arteries as rivers flowing freely. High cholesterol builds up like debris in these rivers, blocking the smooth flow of water (blood) and straining the heart. It's akin to a beaver dam in a stream; the blockage can cause water to overflow or change course, leading to potential devastation downstream. The solution isn't to eliminate all fats but to choose wisely swapping out saturated fats for heart-healthy ones found in fish, nuts, and olive oil.

The Sedentary Lifestyle: The Silent Killer

In today's digital age, sitting has become the new smoking. A sedentary lifestyle is akin to leaving your car idling for hours; it's running, but it's not going anywhere, and it's certainly not doing the engine any favors.

Movement, even in short bursts throughout the day, keeps the heart engine running smoothly and efficiently. Think of it as regular maintenance for your car; without it, the engine starts to run into problems. Swapping elevator rides for stairs or scheduling short walk breaks can kick-start your heart health and keep the engine purring.

Mitigating the Risks

The journey to a healthier heart is not about monumental changes overnight but about small, sustainable shifts in our daily choices. By understanding these risks and taking proactive steps to mitigate them, we can navigate the path to cardiovascular health with confidence. Regular health check-ups, mindful eating, and embracing an active lifestyle are the cornerstones of keeping these risk factors at bay. Remember, every step towards mitigating these risks is a step closer to a healthier, happier heart.

CHAPTER 2

HEART-FRIENDLY FOODS

Embarking on a journey toward heart health is akin to navigating a river: it requires knowledge, skill, and the right provisions. At the heart of this voyage is the food we choose to fuel our bodies with. This chapter is dedicated to identifying the allies and adversaries on our plate, offering a clear guide to foods that cherish our heart and those we're better off without. Just as a captain selects the best equipment for their journey, we must choose our ingredients wisely, ensuring our heart remains robust and resilient against the tides of life.

Recommended Ingredients vs. Avoid Ingredients

RECOMMENDED INGREDIENTS	BENEFITS	AVOID INGREDIENTS	REASONS TO AVOID
Oats and Whole Grains	Rich in fiber, helps lower LDL (bad) cholesterol.	Refined Grains	Lack fiber; can spike blood sugar levels.
Fatty Fish (Salmon, Mackerel, Sardines)	High in omega-3 fatty acids; reduces inflammation and blood clotting.	Processed Meats	High in saturated fat and sodium.
Leafy Greens (Spinach, Kale)	High in vitamins, minerals, and antioxidants; supports blood pressure control.	Trans Fats (Found in some margarines, bakery goods)	Increases risk of heart disease by raising LDL cholesterol.
Nuts and Seeds (Almonds, Chia Seeds)	Source of healthy fats, protein, and fiber; improves heart health markers.	High-Sodium Snacks	Can increase blood pressure; strain on heart health.
Berries and Citrus Fruits	Antioxidant-rich; supports heart health by reducing blood pressure and cholesterol.	Sugary Beverages	High sugar content contributes to obesity and diabetes risk.
Olive Oil	Rich in monounsaturated fats; lowers risk of heart disease and stroke.	Full-Fat Dairy Products	High in saturated fats; can raise LDL cholesterol levels.
Legumes (Beans, Lentils)	Excellent protein source; high in fiber and low in fat.	Deep-Fried Foods	High in unhealthy fats; linked to heart disease risk.
Avocados	Loaded with monounsaturated fats; lowers LDL and raises HDL cholesterol.	Excessive Alcohol	Can lead to high blood pressure, heart failure, and stroke.

This table serves as a compass, guiding you toward heart-friendly foods while steering clear of those that may jeopardize your cardiovascular well-being.

CHAPTER 3
UNDERSTANDING FOOD LABELS

Ever stood in a grocery aisle, a food package in hand, feeling like you're trying to read a foreign language? You're not alone. The maze of numbers and terms on food labels confuses many, leaving us wondering what's truly good for our heart. This chapter is your compass. It's about cracking the code of food labels, turning confusion into clarity. By mastering this skill, you'll be equipped to make choices that favor your heart's health, effortlessly navigating through the marketing noise to the truth that lies in the fine print. Let's demystify those labels together, making every grocery trip a step towards better heart health.

Deciphering Labels

Unlocking the secrets of food labels is like becoming a detective in your own kitchen. Each label holds clues to what's really inside that package, clues crucial for protecting your heart. Here's how you turn from a casual shopper into a savvy nutrition detective, focusing on the essentials: sodium, fats, and sugars.

Step 1: Serving Size and Servings Per Container

Start your investigation with the serving size and servings per container. These numbers are your baseline. They tell you how much of the food is considered a single serving and how many of those servings are in the entire package. Remember, all the nutrient information that follows is based on this serving size, not necessarily the whole package. It's easy to eat more than you think if you're not careful.

Step 2: Sodium - The Stealthy Component

Sodium, essential for body function, can turn into a foe when consumed in excess. High sodium intake is linked to increased blood pressure, a major risk factor for heart disease. Your target? Look for foods with less than 200 mg of sodium per serving. Consider anything above 400 mg a red flag.

Step 3: Fats - The Good, The Bad, and The Ugly

Not all fats are villains in the story of heart health. Trans fats and saturated fats are the culprits you want to avoid, as they can raise bad cholesterol levels and increase the risk of heart disease. On the label, aim for products with low saturated fats (less than 2g per serving) and zero trans fats. Instead, look for unsaturated fats, which can be good for your heart.

Step 4: Sugars - The Sweet Deception

Sugars, especially added sugars, can sneak into foods you wouldn't expect, contributing to weight gain and cardiovascular problems. On the label, check the total sugars, but give extra attention to added sugars. The American Heart Association recommends no more than 36 grams of added sugar per day for men and 25 grams for women. Choose foods with little to no added sugars to keep your heart beating happily.

Decoding Activity

Grab a food item from your pantry, preferably something you consume often. Apply these steps to its label. What did you find? Were there any surprises? This activity isn't just an eye-opener; it's a step towards making heart-healthier choices every day.

By becoming proficient in label literacy, you equip yourself with the knowledge to choose foods that nourish your heart and support your overall health. With each grocery trip, you're not just filling your cart; you're investing in your heart's well-being.

American Measurement Units: Navigating the Kitchen's Language

Cooking is not just an art; it's a science where precision matters, especially when you're trying to keep your heart happy and healthy. One of the first challenges you might face in this science is understanding the American system of measurement. Cups, teaspoons, tablespoons—these units may seem like simple kitchen terms, but they are crucial tools in the recipe for a heart-healthy lifestyle. Getting familiar with these measures and how to convert them is like learning a new language, one that opens up a world of culinary possibilities while keeping your heart's health in check. Let's dive into the basics, transforming you into a fluent speaker of the kitchen's language, ensuring every pinch, dash, and scoop contributes to your wellness.

Cups, Teaspoons, Tablespoons: The Essentials

In the heart of American kitchens, recipes speak a language of cups for volume, teaspoons, and tablespoons for smaller measures. A cup, often used for both liquids and solids, is the cornerstone of cooking measurements. Imagine it as a standard coffee mug—a size most are familiar with. For smaller ingredients, we turn to teaspoons and tablespoons. Picture a teaspoon as the size of the tip of your thumb, while a tablespoon is about the size of a whole walnut.

Conversion Made Simple

Conversion between these units might seem daunting, but it's simpler than you think. Three teaspoons equal one tablespoon, making it easy to switch between them when you're a teaspoon short. Need more? Remember that sixteen tablespoons make up one cup. This knowledge is like having a secret key, unlocking the ability to effortlessly adjust recipes to your heart's content.

Measuring Liquids vs. Solids

Accuracy in measuring liquids and solids can make or break a recipe. For liquids, use a clear measuring cup with a spout, filling it to eye level for precision. When it comes to solids like flour or sugar, spoon them into the measuring cup without packing, then level off with a knife's flat edge. This technique ensures you're not adding more to your mix than your heart desires.

Quick Reference Guide
Here's a quick guide to keep handy:

- 3 teaspoons (tsp) = 1 tablespoon (tbsp)
- 16 tablespoons (tbsp) = 1 cup (c)
- 2 cups (c) = 1 pint (pt)
- 4 cups (c) = 1 quart (qt)
- 4 quarts (qt) = 1 gallon (gal)

Tips for Accurate Measuring

- Always use the right tool for the measure: liquid measuring cups for liquids, dry cups for dry ingredients.
- For ingredients that can settle, like flour, fluff it up before spooning it into the measuring cup.
- Invest in a kitchen scale for the utmost precision, an invaluable tool for those dedicated to heart health.

Understanding and using these measurement units correctly is more than just following recipes; it's about taking control of your diet and, by extension, your heart health. With this guide, you're now equipped to measure with confidence, making each meal a calculated step towards a healthier heart.

CHAPTER 4

MEAL PLANNING FOR HEART HEALTH

Ever found yourself hungry, staring into the fridge, and reaching for the first thing that looks good, only to realize it's packed with salt, sugar, or unhealthy fats? It's a common tale that often ends with regret and a promise to do better next time. Here's where the magic of meal planning steps in, transforming chaos into harmony. Meal planning isn't just about saving time; it's a strategic ally in the quest for a heart-healthy lifestyle. By planning your meals, you take control, ensuring each dish supports your heart's health, rather than challenging it. Let's turn the page on last-minute, unhealthy choices and welcome a future where every meal is a step towards a healthier heart.

Meal Planning for Heart Health

Planning Strategies

The art of meal planning is akin to drafting the blueprint for this journey, ensuring that every meal not only satisfies your taste buds but also nourishes your heart.

Imagine your plate as a colorful canvas, each color representing a different nutrient your heart craves. Start by painting with broad strokes, incorporating a variety of colors through vegetables, fruits, whole grains, lean proteins, and healthy fats. This diversity is not just about aesthetics; it ensures your heart gets a broad spectrum of nutrients, each playing a unique role in maintaining its health.

Consider the following template for a week's meal plan, inspired by the list of recipes provided in this book. Each day is designed to introduce a balanced mix of nutrients, flavors, and textures, keeping your meals exciting and heart healthy.

Monday to Sunday: A Heart-Healthy Meal Plan Canvas

- **Monday:** Breakfast: Antioxidant Green Smoothie Lunch: Mediterranean Quinoa Salad Dinner: Baked Salmon with Avocado Sauce Snacks: Carrot Sticks and Hummus
- **Tuesday:** Breakfast: Oat and Apple Porridge with Cinnamon Lunch: Whole Wheat Spring Pasta Dinner: Vegetarian Chili with Quinoa and Black Beans Snacks: Baked Kale Chips
- **Wednesday:** Breakfast: Whole Blueberry Muffins Lunch: Grilled Chicken Breast with Avocado Salsa Dinner: Whole Wheat Spaghetti with Avocado Pesto Snacks: Steamed Edamame with Sea Salt
- **Thursday:** Breakfast: Avocado and Poached Egg Toast Lunch: Barley with Cherry Tomatoes and Arugula Dinner: Stuffed Chicken Breast with Spinach and Ricotta Snacks: Spiced Toasted Nuts

- **Friday:** Breakfast: Yogurt, Fruit, and Nut Parfait Lunch: Lemon Thyme Chicken with Quinoa Dinner: Vegetarian Zucchini and Ricotta Lasagna Snacks: Oat and Banana Muffins
- **Saturday:** Breakfast: Banana and Oat Pancakes Lunch: Greek Chickpea Salad Dinner: Baked Sea Bass with Olives and Cherry Tomatoes Snacks: Avocado and Tomato Crostini
- **Sunday:** Breakfast: Protein Coffee Smoothie Lunch: Bulgur, Cucumber, and Mint Salad Dinner: Peppered Beef Tenderloin with Arugula Salad Snacks: Homemade Energy Bars

Seasonality and Shopping Smart

To keep your meal plan both economical and environmentally friendly, lean into the rhythm of the seasons. Choosing fruits and vegetables that are in season not only enhances the flavor of your meals but also ensures you're getting the nutrients at their peak. When shopping, arm yourself with a list based on your meal plan, steering clear of impulse buys that might derail your heart-healthy goals.

Customizing Your Meal Plan

The beauty of meal planning lies in its flexibility. Feel free to swap ingredients based on availability or personal preference, keeping the nutritional balance intact. If you're short on time during the week, consider batch cooking or preparing some components of your meals ahead of time. This not only saves time but also reduces the temptation to opt for less healthy convenience foods.

Through careful planning and a dash of creativity, meal planning becomes not just a tool for heart health but a doorway to a richer, more flavorful life. Each meal is a step towards not just a healthier heart, but a happier, more vibrant you.

Meal Preparation: Your Blueprint for Heart-Healthy Eating

In the rhythm of modern life, finding the time to cook every meal from scratch is a challenge few of us can meet. Yet, the secret to sustaining a heart-healthy diet lies not in the high-stakes balancing act of daily cooking but in the simple, smart strategy of meal preparation. Imagine opening your fridge to find a week's worth of heart-friendly meals ready to go. This isn't just convenient; it's your ticket to consistently nourishing your body with the right foods. Let's dive into how you can transform your kitchen habits with meal prep, making heart-healthy eating a natural part of your routine.

The Foundation: Building a Heart-Healthy Pantry

Start with your pantry. Stocking up on whole grains like quinoa, brown rice, and farro gives you a versatile base for many meals. Canned beans, no-salt-added tomatoes, and a variety of spices can turn these staples into flavorful dishes without the need for added sodium or unhealthy fats. Including a range of nuts, seeds, and dried fruits allows for quick, nutritious snacking options or enhancements to meals. Remember, a well-prepared pantry is your best ally.

Batch Cooking: The Time-Saver

Batch cooking is your efficiency hack. It means cooking larger quantities of a meal at once, then dividing it into portions for the week. Consider making a large pot of chili using lean ground turkey or a big batch of quinoa salad with plenty of veggies. These can serve as main meals or sides throughout the week. When batch cooking, focus on recipes that freeze well, ensuring you always have a heart-healthy option on hand, even on your busiest days.

Storing Tips: Keeping It Fresh

Proper storage is crucial for maintaining the freshness and nutritional value of your prepped meals. Invest in a set of high-quality, airtight containers. Glass containers are ideal for storing meals in the fridge, as they don't harbor bacteria or odors and can go straight into the oven for reheating. For freezing, ensure containers are freezer-safe to prevent freezer burn. Labeling meals with the date of preparation can help you keep track of what's fresh and what needs to be eaten soon.

Efficient Tools: The Right Gear

A few key kitchen tools can make meal prep significantly easier. A good set of knives, a large cutting board, and a food processor can cut down on prep time. Slow cookers and pressure cookers are excellent for making large batches of stews, soups, and grains with minimal effort. Lastly, don't underestimate the power of a good blender for quick smoothies and sauces.

Simple Prep Ideas: From Novice to Pro

For those new to meal prep, start simple. Try prepping just one meal type for the week, like breakfast. Oatmeal cups, breakfast burritos, or smoothie packs are great starters. As you become more comfortable, expand to preparing lunches or dinners. Grilled chicken breasts can be a versatile protein for salads, wraps, or paired with vegetables and a grain for a complete meal. Roasted vegetables, prepared in bulk, can be a colorful, nutritious addition to any meal.

Meal preparation is more than just a time-saving strategy; it's a commitment to your heart's health and your overall well-being. With these tips and a bit of planning, you'll find that eating heart-healthy meals becomes a seamless, enjoyable part of your week.

CHAPTER 5

TIPS FOR HEALTHY COOKING

Imagine a favorite dish, perhaps one passed down through generations, rich in flavor but equally rich in ingredients that make your heart work harder than it should. Now picture this dish reimagined, its essence preserved yet transformed into a beacon of heart health. This is not just a dream; it's the very real journey we embark on in this chapter. Here, we bridge the gap between the love of cooking and the essentials of heart health. By exploring cooking methods that boost heart wellness and learning to substitute ingredients with healthier alternatives, we redefine what comfort food means. Welcome to a world where every meal not only delights your taste buds but also nourishes your heart.

Cooking Techniques for a Healthy Heart

In the quest for heart health, how we cook can be just as important as what we cook. Moving away from methods that rely heavily on added fats and towards those that preserve the integrity and nutrients of food not only benefits our heart but also introduces us to a world of vibrant flavors and textures. Let's explore cooking techniques that keep your heart in mind, along with the why and how that makes them stand out.

Steaming: The Gentle Powerhouse
Steaming is a champion of heart health, gently coaxing out the flavors of vegetables, fish, and even chicken without the need for oil. This method keeps cholesterol levels in check and preserves the natural nutrients and colors of food. A simple steamed salmon with a sprinkle of herbs and a dash of lemon zest can turn a weeknight dinner into a heart-healthy feast.

Baking: Beyond Bread
Baking isn't just for sweets and breads; it's a fantastic way to prepare meals in a heart-friendly manner. Unlike frying, baking doesn't submerge food in fat. A tray of mixed vegetables drizzled with olive oil and herbs, or chicken breasts marinated in a blend of spices and baked to perfection showcases how this method can be both simple and spectacularly healthy.

Grilling: Flavor Without the Guilt
Grilling imparts a smoky flavor to foods, from vegetables to lean meats, without the need for added fats. It allows fat to drip away from the food, reducing calorie intake while keeping the heart-healthy essence intact. A grilled vegetable kebab or a piece of fish over the grill can be a delightful way to enjoy the richness of flavors guilt-free.

Ingredient Substitutions for Healthier Eating

Transforming a meal from a guilty pleasure to a heart-healthy delight often starts with swapping out ingredients for more nutritious options. These substitutions not only keep your dishes delicious but also boost their health benefits. Here's a guide to making smarter, heart-friendly choices in the kitchen.

UNHEALTHY INGREDIENT	HEALTHY ALTERNATIVE	HEALTH BENEFITS
Butter	Avocado or Olive Oil	Reduces saturated fat, rich in monounsaturated fats
White Rice	Quinoa or Brown Rice	Higher in fiber and nutrients, lower glycemic index
Cream	Greek Yogurt	Lower fat, higher in protein
Sugar	Honey or Maple Syrup	Less processed, contains antioxidants
Salt	Herbs and Spices	Reduces sodium intake, adds flavor without the health risks

Incorporating these substitutions doesn't just tweak the nutritional content of your meals—it opens up a new dimension of flavors and textures. Experimenting with these swaps, like using avocado in place of butter in your baking or seasoning with herbs instead of salt, can introduce a refreshing twist to your favorite dishes without sacrificing taste.

CHAPTER 6
ADAPTING RECIPES FOR THE HEART

Picture a classic, richly sauced lasagna, a staple of Sunday family dinners, now reimagined with whole grain noodles, lean ground turkey, and a rainbow of roasted vegetables. It's still the lasagna that pulled everyone to the table, only now it pulls double duty, nourishing your heart and soul. Together, we'll journey through the alchemy of recipe adaptation, making each beloved dish a tribute to both tradition and well-being. Welcome to the heart of healthy eating, where every recipe is a love letter to your heart.

Modifying Existing Recipes

Transforming your beloved recipes into heart-healthy masterpieces doesn't mean sacrificing the flavors that make your taste buds sing. It's about making smart swaps and tweaks that keep the essence of the dish alive while enhancing its nutritional profile. Let's embark on a culinary quest to revamp your favorites, turning them into treasures for both your palate and your heart.

Analyzing Recipes for Unhealthy Components
Start with a detective's eye, examining each ingredient for hidden culprits that might be sneaking extra sodium, saturated fats, or sugars into your meals. For example, consider a traditional creamy soup. Its richness often comes from heavy cream, which packs a hefty dose of saturated fat.

Making Substitutions
The art of substitution is where creativity meets health. In our creamy soup scenario, swap out heavy cream for a blend of low-fat milk and pureed white beans. Not only does this dramatically reduce the fat content, but it also introduces fiber and protein, turning your soup into a heart-friendly comfort food.

Before-and-After Recipe Comparison
Imagine a classic beef stew, traditionally reliant on fatty cuts of meat and thickened with refined flour. By replacing the beef with lean cuts or even heart-healthy proteins like chickpeas, and thickening the stew with pureed vegetables, we maintain the soul-warming depth of flavor while significantly improving its health profile.

Encouraging Experimentation
The journey to heart-healthy eating is personal and ripe for experimentation. Take the modified beef stew recipe for a test drive, adjusting spices and herbs to suit your taste. Feedback from these taste tests can be invaluable, helping you fine-tune the recipe to perfection.

Maintaining Flavor While Boosting Nutritional Value

Spices and herbs are your best friends in this endeavor. They add a complexity of flavor without the need for excess salt or fat. Fresh herbs, citrus zest, and aromatic spices can transform a dish from good to unforgettable, all while keeping it squarely in the heart-healthy category.

By embracing these modifications, you create meals that don't just feed the body but also protect the heart. Each recipe becomes a testament to the possibility of enjoying the full spectrum of flavors life has to offer, without compromising on health. This approach to cooking not only nourishes the heart but also enriches the culinary experience, making each meal a celebration of taste and well-being.

Practical Examples: Heart-Healthy Recipe Transformations

Transforming your favorite dishes into heart-healthy meals doesn't mean sacrificing flavor or tradition; it means enhancing them. By making smart substitutions, we can turn any meal into a nutrient-rich, heart-friendly version that still satisfies our taste buds. Let's dive into some practical examples, showing just how versatile and delicious these adaptations can be. From the first meal of the day to a comforting evening dinner, these reimagined recipes demonstrate that eating for your heart can be both joyful and delicious.

Breakfast: Oatmeal Banana Pancakes

Original: Traditional pancakes often come loaded with refined flour and sugar, topped with butter and syrup. Heart-Healthy Version: Swap in whole oats ground into flour and ripe bananas for natural sweetness. Cook them in a non-stick pan with a drizzle of heart-healthy olive oil. Serve with a dollop of low-fat Greek yogurt and fresh berries instead of syrup.

Lunch: Mediterranean Quinoa Salad

Original: A creamy pasta salad, typically dressed in mayonnaise and loaded with processed meats. Heart-Healthy Version: Use quinoa as a base for its high protein and fiber content. Add a rainbow of vegetables like cherry tomatoes, cucumbers, and bell peppers. Toss with a dressing made from extra virgin olive oil and lemon juice, and top with a sprinkle of feta cheese for a tangy finish.

Dinner: Veggie-Loaded Turkey Chili

Original: Classic chili recipes often rely on fatty ground beef and minimal vegetables. Heart-Healthy Version: Choose lean ground turkey as your protein and double the usual amount of vegetables by adding zucchini, bell peppers, and carrots. Use low-sodium canned tomatoes and beans to control the salt content. Spice it up with fresh herbs and spices rather than pre-packaged mixes to keep it flavorful and heart healthy.

Snack: Avocado Chocolate Mousse

Original: A dessert laden with heavy cream and chocolate. Heart-Healthy Version: Blend ripe avocados for creaminess, adding cocoa powder for that chocolatey flavor and a touch of maple syrup for sweetness. Avocado brings healthy fats to your dessert, making it indulgent yet beneficial for your heart.

These examples showcase the endless possibilities of recipe adaptation. By choosing whole grains, leaning on fruits and vegetables, selecting lean proteins, and embracing healthy fats, we can recreate any dish into a heart-healthy masterpiece. Each modification not only brings us closer to our health goals but also expands our culinary horizons, proving that healthy eating is anything but boring.

CHAPTER 7
IMPROVING CARDIOVASCULAR WELLNESS

The power of diet over our heart's health cannot be overstated. Every bite we take can be a step towards fortifying our heart or an inadvertent nudge towards its decline. This chapter unravels the profound impact of dietary choices on cardiovascular wellness, illuminating the path to a heart that thrives rather than just survives. Emerging research and countless success stories have illuminated the potential to not only manage but transform our heart health through what we eat. Here, we delve into managing crucial dietary components—cholesterol, triglycerides, and homocysteine—each playing a pivotal role in our cardiovascular system's wellbeing. With each page, we embark on a journey towards a heart that's not just beating but flourishing.

Cholesterol, Triglycerides, and Homocysteine: Keys to a Healthy Heart

Understanding the trio of cholesterol, triglycerides, and homocysteine is like unlocking the secrets to a healthy heart. These markers, often whispered about in the corridors of clinics, play starring roles in the story of our cardiovascular health. But fear not, as the power to influence these levels lies within our grasp, nestled in the choices we make at the dining table. Let's demystify these terms and learn how a mindful diet can become our heart's strongest ally.

Cholesterol: The Double-Edged Sword

Cholesterol travels through our blood, but not all cholesterol is created equal. There's LDL (low-density lipoprotein) cholesterol, often dubbed 'bad' because it can build up and clog arteries. Then there's HDL (high-density lipoprotein) cholesterol, the 'good' counterpart, which helps remove LDL from the arteries. Balancing these levels is crucial. Favor foods rich in omega-3 fatty acids, such as salmon, flaxseeds, and walnuts, which can help raise HDL levels. Incorporate plenty of fruits, vegetables, and whole grains to keep LDL levels in check.

Triglycerides: The Fatty Balancers

Triglycerides are a type of fat found in the blood. High levels, often a result of excess calorie intake, can lead to coronary artery disease. The secret to managing triglycerides? A diet low in sugars and refined carbs. Focus on whole foods like lean proteins, leafy greens, and whole grains. Avocados and olive oil, with their heart-healthy fats, can also help maintain a balance.

Homocysteine: The Silent Alarm

Homocysteine, an amino acid in the blood, can hint at heart health issues when levels spike. High homocysteine is often linked to a deficiency in B vitamins. Thus, to manage homocysteine levels, turn to B-vitamin-rich foods. Leafy greens, fortified cereals, and legumes are excellent sources of folate (B9), while eggs, dairy, and meat provide ample B12 and B6.

Bringing It All Together

Taming these markers doesn't demand a culinary revolution but rather thoughtful choices. Swap out processed foods for whole, nutrient-dense options. Embrace variety to cover all your nutritional bases, ensuring each meal is an opportunity to support your heart. By understanding and adjusting our diets to manage cholesterol, triglycerides, and homocysteine, we wield the power to steer our heart health towards a brighter, healthier future.

Risk Reduction Strategies

In the quest for a heart that beats strongly into the future, small shifts in our daily lives can pave the path to profound wellness. The journey to reducing cardiovascular risk doesn't require a leap into the unknown but rather, the adoption of simple, sustainable steps. Each choice we make, from the foods we eat to the moments we move, weaves a tapestry of protection around our most vital organ. Let's navigate through actionable strategies that are not only manageable but can seamlessly blend into the rhythm of our everyday lives, ensuring our heart's vitality is not just a goal, but a reality.

Diet: The Foundation of Heart Health

1. **Embrace Whole Grains:** Swap refined grains for whole grain alternatives. Start with one meal a day, gradually increasing until whole grains are your go-to.

2. **Fruits and Vegetables Rainbow:** Aim to fill half your plate with a variety of colors at every meal. Not only does this ensure a wide range of nutrients, but it also helps in reducing cravings for unhealthy options.

3. **Lean on Lean Proteins:** Choose fish, poultry, beans, and legumes more often than red meats. Incorporating fish like salmon or mackerel twice a week can boost heart-healthy omega-3 fatty acids.

Physical Activity: Every Step Counts

1. **Incorporate Movement into Your Routine:** Start with a 10-minute walk daily, gradually increasing the duration. Finding activities, you enjoy can turn exercise from a chore into a highlight of your day.

2. **Break Up Sitting Time:** Set reminders to stand or walk for a few minutes every hour. Small changes, like taking the stairs instead of the elevator, can add up.

Stress Management: A Calm Heart

1. **Mindful Moments:** Dedicate a few minutes each day to mindfulness or meditation. Starting or ending your day with a mindfulness exercise can help in managing stress levels.

2. **Find Your Joy:** Engage in hobbies and activities that bring you happiness. Whether it's reading, gardening, or crafting, these can serve as effective stress reducers.

Sleep: The Unsung Hero of Heart Health

1. **Establish a Routine:** Aim for 7-9 hours of sleep by going to bed and waking up at the same time daily. A consistent sleep schedule supports heart health.

2. **Create a Restful Environment:** Ensure your bedroom is conducive to sleep—cool, dark, and quiet. Consider routines that help signal to your body it's time to wind down, like reading or a warm bath.

CHAPTER 8

FUNDAMENTALS OF MACRONUTRIENTS AND MICRONUTRIENTS

Building a strong, resilient heart is much like constructing a house. Just as a house needs a variety of materials — bricks, beams, glass, and nails — our hearts require a diverse mix of nutrients to function optimally. Macronutrients are the beams and bricks, providing the structure and energy, while micronutrients are the nails and glass, small but essential for holding everything together and ensuring it works as it should. This chapter delves into the vital roles these nutritional components play in heart health, highlighting how the right balance can fortify our cardiovascular system.

Importance of Macronutrients

Carbohydrates, Proteins, and Fats: The Cornerstones of Heart Health

Carbohydrates are often misunderstood, with many fearing they are inherently bad. However, they are the primary energy source for our body, including the heart. The key is choosing high-quality carbs found in whole grains, fruits, and vegetables. These foods are not only rich in energy but also in fiber, which helps manage blood sugar levels and reduce cholesterol, protecting the heart.

Proteins are the building blocks of life, essential for repairing and building tissues, including heart muscle. Opting for lean sources of protein, such as fish, poultry, legumes, and nuts, can support heart health by providing essential nutrients without the excess saturated fats found in redder meats.

Fats have long been villainized, but they are crucial for overall health, including heart function. The focus should be on unsaturated fats found in olive oil, avocados, and nuts. These fats help reduce bad cholesterol levels and provide anti-inflammatory benefits, protecting the heart against disease.

Visual aids, such as charts, can help distinguish between healthy and unhealthy sources of these macronutrients. For example, a graph might illustrate the difference in saturated fat content between a serving of salmon and a serving of processed meat, underscoring the importance of making heart-healthy choices.

Incorporating a balanced mix of these macronutrients into our diet lays the foundation for a heart that not only beats but thrives. By focusing on quality and variety, we can ensure our heart has all it needs to support us, keeping the rhythm of life vibrant and strong.

Benefits of Micronutrients

Just as a masterpiece painting relies on a palette of varied hues, our heart's health flourishes on a spectrum of micronutrients. Vitamins and minerals, though required in smaller amounts than macronutrients, are pivotal in orchestrating a symphony of physiological functions that safeguard cardiovascular well-being. Magnesium, for instance, acts as a conductor, regulating heart rhythm and blood pressure, while antioxidants like vitamin C and E play the vigilant protectors, shielding our cells from damage. Omega-3 fatty acids, found abundantly in fatty fish, chia seeds, and walnuts, are like the harmonious chords reducing inflammation and preventing clot formations.

Incorporating these vital nutrients into our diet can be as simple as adding a splash of color to our plates. Spinach, kale, and other leafy greens are not only rich in fiber but also a treasure trove of heart-friendly magnesium, potassium, and calcium. Berries, with their vibrant colors, are loaded with antioxidants. By consciously choosing foods rich in these nutrients, we weave a tapestry of protection for our heart.

Balancing the Diet

Crafting a diet that sings to the heart involves a delicate balance of macronutrients and micronutrients, much like composing a melody where every note has its place. A day's menu might start with a breakfast of oatmeal topped with berries and chia seeds, blending complex carbohydrates, antioxidants, and omega-3s. Lunch could be a quinoa salad with mixed vegetables, avocados, and grilled chicken, offering a mix of proteins, healthy fats, and a spectrum of vitamins and minerals. For dinner, a piece of salmon with a side of steamed broccoli and sweet potatoes rounds off the day with a boost of omega-3s, fiber, and beta-carotene. This template serves as a starting point, encouraging personalization to cater to individual tastes and nutritional needs. The key is variety, ensuring a colorful and diverse intake of foods that collectively contribute to a heart-healthy diet.

CHAPTER 9
BREAKFAST

1. ANTIOXIDANT GREEN SMOOTHIE

Introduction:
Kickstart your day with this Antioxidant Green Smoothie, a vibrant blend of nutrients and flavors. This smoothie combines the creamy texture of banana and Greek yogurt with the fresh taste of spinach and blueberries, offering a delicious way to get your daily dose of antioxidants.

PREPARATION TIME: 5 MINUTES
COOKING TIME: 0 MINUTES
TOTAL TIME: 5 MINUTES
DIFFICULTY: EASY
SERVINGS: 1

PROCEDURE:
1. Add the spinach, banana, blueberries, Greek yogurt, and almond milk to a blender.
2. Blend on high speed until the mixture is smooth.
3. Add the chia seeds and pulse a few times to mix.
4. Pour the smoothie into a glass and serve immediately.

INGREDIENTS:
- 1 cup fresh spinach
- 1 ripe banana
- ½ cup frozen blueberries
- ½ cup low-fat Greek yogurt
- ½ cup almond milk
- 1 tablespoon chia seeds

NUTRITIONAL VALUES (APPROXIMATE):
Calories: 300 kcal; **Carbohydrates:** 50 g; **Proteins:** 15 g; **Fats:** 5 g; **Cholesterol:** 5 mg; **Sodium:** 120 mg; **Fiber:** 8 g.

2. OAT AND APPLE PORRIDGE WITH CINNAMON

Introduction:
Warm and comforting, this Oat and Apple Porridge with Cinnamon is the perfect way to warm up on a chilly morning. The sweetness of apple paired with the aromatic cinnamon and the heartiness of oats makes this breakfast both satisfying and heart-healthy.

PREPARATION TIME: 5 MINUTES
COOKING TIME: 15 MINUTES
TOTAL TIME: 20 MINUTES
DIFFICULTY: EASY
SERVINGS: 1

PROCEDURE:
1. In a medium saucepan, bring the almond milk to a boil.
2. Add the oats, diced apple, cinnamon, and sea salt. Reduce the heat to low.
3. Simmer for 10-15 minutes, stirring occasionally, until the oats are cooked and creamy.
4. Transfer to a bowl and top with chopped walnuts and a drizzle of honey if desired.
5. Serve warm and enjoy.

INGREDIENTS:
- ½ cup whole oats
- 1 cup almond milk
- 1 diced apple
- ½ teaspoon ground cinnamon
- A pinch of sea salt
- ¼ cup chopped walnuts
- 1 tablespoon honey (optional)

NUTRITIONAL VALUES (APPROXIMATE):
Calories: 350 kcal; **Carbohydrates:** 55 g; **Proteins:** 10 g; **Fats:** 12 g; **Cholesterol:** 0 mg; **Sodium:** 200 mg; **Fiber:** 8 g

3. WHOLE BLUEBERRY MUFFINS

Introduction:
Discover the joy of baking with these Whole Blueberry Muffins, a treat that's as nutritious as it is delicious. Bursting with fresh blueberries and made with whole wheat flour and Greek yogurt, these muffins offer a healthier alternative to satisfy your morning cravings or afternoon snack time.

PREPARATION TIME: 10 MINUTES
COOKING TIME: 20 MINUTES
TOTAL TIME: 30 MINUTES
DIFFICULTY: MEDIUM
SERVINGS: 1

INGREDIENTS:

- ¾ cup whole wheat flour
- ½ cup fresh blueberries
- ¼ cup low-fat Greek yogurt
- 1 egg
- 2 tablespoons honey
- 2 tablespoons canola oil
- 1 teaspoon baking powder
- ½ teaspoon vanilla extract

PROCEDURE:

1. Preheat your oven to 375°F (190°C) and line a muffin tin with paper liners or lightly grease it.
2. In a large bowl, combine the whole wheat flour and baking powder.
3. In another bowl, whisk together the egg, Greek yogurt, honey, canola oil, and vanilla extract until well combined.
4. Add the wet ingredients to the dry ingredients, stirring until just combined. Be careful not to overmix.
5. Gently fold in the blueberries.
6. Divide the batter evenly among the muffin cups, filling each about ⅔ full.
7. Bake for 18-20 minutes, or until a toothpick inserted into the center of a muffin comes out clean.
8. Let the muffins cool in the pan for 5 minutes, then transfer them to a wire rack to cool completely.

NUTRITIONAL VALUES (APPROXIMATE, PER MUFFIN):
Calories: 180 kcal; **Carbohydrates:** 24 g; **Proteins:** 4 g; **Fats:** 8 g; **Cholesterol:** 30 mg; **Sodium:** 120 mg; **Fiber:** 3 g

4. AVOCADO AND POACHED EGG TOAST

Introduction:
Elevate your breakfast routine with this nutritious and satisfying Avocado and Poached Egg Toast. Combining the creamy texture of ripe avocado with the delicate flavors of a poached egg, this dish is a perfect blend of taste and health. It's a simple yet elegant choice that's sure to start your day on a high note.

PREPARATION TIME: 5 MINUTES
COOKING TIME: 5 MINUTES
TOTAL TIME: 10 MINUTES
DIFFICULTY: EASY
SERVINGS: 1

INGREDIENTS:

- 1 slice whole grain bread
- 1 ripe avocado
- 1 egg
- 1 tablespoon sunflower seeds
- Black pepper, to taste
- A pinch of sea salt

PROCEDURE:

1. Toast the whole grain bread to your liking.
2. Meanwhile, bring a pot of water to a gentle simmer. Crack the egg into a cup and gently slide it into the simmering water. Poach the egg for 3-4 minutes, or until the whites are set but the yolk remains runny.
3. While the egg is poaching, mash the ripe avocado in a bowl. Season with a pinch of sea salt and black pepper.
4. Spread the mashed avocado evenly over the toasted bread.
5. Carefully remove the poached egg from the water with a slotted spoon and drain it on a paper towel. Place the egg on top of the avocado spread.
6. Sprinkle sunflower seeds over the top for a crunchy finish. Add an additional sprinkle of sea salt and black pepper, to taste.

NUTRITIONAL VALUES (APPROXIMATE):
Calories: 320 kcal; **Carbohydrates:** 30 g; **Proteins:** 12 g; **Fats:** 18 g; **Cholesterol:** 186 mg; **Sodium:** 200 mg; **Fiber:** 7 g.

5. BAKED VEGETABLE FRITTATA

Introduction:
Start your day with a burst of color and flavor with the Baked Vegetable Frittata. This dish is not only easy to prepare but is also packed with nutrients from a variety of vegetables and the wholesomeness of eggs. Perfect for a leisurely weekend breakfast or a quick weekday meal, it's a versatile recipe that you can adapt to whatever veggies you have on hand.

PREPARATION TIME: 10 MINUTES
COOKING TIME: 25 MINUTES
TOTAL TIME: 35 MINUTES
DIFFICULTY: MEDIUM
SERVINGS: 1

INGREDIENTS:

- 2 eggs
- ¼ cup chopped spinach
- ¼ cup diced tomatoes
- ¼ cup diced bell peppers
- 2 tablespoons diced onions
- 2 tablespoons low-fat feta cheese, crumbled
- Mixed herbs (such as basil, oregano, and thyme), to taste

PROCEDURE:

1. Preheat the oven to 375°F (190°C). Grease a small baking dish or oven-safe skillet.
2. In a bowl, whisk the eggs until well beaten. Add the chopped spinach, diced tomatoes, bell peppers, onions, crumbled feta cheese, and mixed herbs. Stir to combine.
3. Pour the egg and vegetable mixture into the prepared baking dish.
4. Bake in the preheated oven for 20-25 minutes, or until the eggs are set and the top is lightly golden.
5. Remove from the oven and let it cool for a few minutes before serving.

NUTRITIONAL VALUES (APPROXIMATE):

Calories: 220 kcal; **Carbohydrates:** 10 g; **Proteins:** 14 g; **Fats:** 14 g; **Cholesterol:** 370 mg; **Sodium:** 320 mg; **Fiber:** 2 g

6. BANANA AND OAT PANCAKES

Introduction:
Indulge in the naturally sweet and satisfying Banana and Oat Pancakes, a wholesome start to your day. These pancakes are not only fluffy and delicious but also pack a nutritious punch with whole oats and ripe bananas. Perfect for a weekend brunch or a special breakfast, they're sure to be a hit with everyone.

PREPARATION TIME: 10 MINUTES
COOKING TIME: 10 MINUTES
TOTAL TIME: 20 MINUTES
DIFFICULTY: EASY
SERVINGS: 1

PROCEDURE:

1. In a blender, combine the whole oats, ripe banana, eggs, almond milk, baking powder, and cinnamon. Blend until the mixture is smooth.
2. Heat a non-stick skillet over medium heat and add a small amount of coconut oil to coat the bottom.
3. Pour ¼ cup of the pancake batter onto the skillet for each pancake. Cook until bubbles form on the surface and the edges look set, about 2-3 minutes.
4. Flip the pancakes carefully and cook for another 2 minutes or until golden brown and cooked through.
5. Repeat with the remaining batter, adding more coconut oil to the skillet as needed.
6. Serve the pancakes warm with your favorite toppings, such as fresh fruit, yogurt, or a drizzle of honey.

INGREDIENTS:

- ½ cup whole oats
- 1 ripe banana
- 2 eggs
- ¼ cup almond milk
- ½ teaspoon baking powder
- ¼ teaspoon cinnamon
- Coconut oil, for cooking

NUTRITIONAL VALUES (APPROXIMATE, PER SERVING WITHOUT TOPPINGS):

Calories: 350 kcal; **Carbohydrates:** 45 g; **Proteins:** 15 g; **Fats:** 12 g; **Cholesterol:** 370 mg; **Sodium:** 150 mg; **Fiber:** 6 g;.

7. YOGURT, FRUIT, AND NUT PARFAIT

Introduction:

Brighten your morning with a Yogurt, Fruit, and Nut Parfait, a layered delight that's as beautiful as it is beneficial for your heart health. This parfait combines the creamy texture of Greek yogurt with the sweet and tangy flavors of fresh fruits, topped with a crunchy mix of nuts and granola. It's a perfect breakfast for those on the go or anyone looking for a refreshing and nutritious start to their day.

PREPARATION TIME: 5 MINUTES
COOKING TIME: 0 MINUTES
TOTAL TIME: 5 MINUTES
DIFFICULTY: EASY
SERVINGS: 1

INGREDIENTS:

- ¾ cup low-fat Greek yogurt
- ½ cup fresh blueberries
- ½ cup sliced strawberries
- ¼ cup low-sugar granola
- 2 tablespoons chopped nuts (almonds, walnuts, or pecans)

PROCEDURE:

1. In a serving glass or bowl, start by layering half of the Greek yogurt at the bottom.
2. Add a layer of blueberries, followed by a layer of sliced strawberries.
3. Sprinkle half of the granola and chopped nuts over the strawberries.
4. Repeat the layers with the remaining yogurt, blueberries, strawberries, granola, and nuts.
5. Serve immediately or refrigerate for up to an hour before serving for a chilled parfait.

NUTRITIONAL VALUES (APPROXIMATE):

Calories: 300 kcal; **Carbohydrates:** 35 g; **Proteins:** 20 g; **Fats:** 10 g; **Cholesterol:** 10 mg; **Sodium:** 85 mg; **Fiber:** 5 g

8. PROTEIN COFFEE SMOOTHIE

Introduction:

Merge your morning coffee ritual with your protein intake in this innovative Protein Coffee Smoothie. Ideal for those on-the-go mornings or when you need an extra boost post-workout, this smoothie combines the rich taste of cold brew coffee with the creamy texture of banana and almond milk, all while packing a protein punch.

PREPARATION TIME: 5 MINUTES
COOKING TIME: 0 MINUTES
TOTAL TIME: 5 MINUTES
DIFFICULTY: EASY
SERVINGS: 1

INGREDIENTS:

- ½ cup cold brew coffee
- ½ cup almond milk
- 1 scoop neutral protein powder
- 1 frozen banana
- 1 tablespoon cocoa powder
- 1 tablespoon honey (optional)

PROCEDURE:

1. Place the cold brew coffee, almond milk, protein powder, frozen banana, cocoa powder, and honey (if using) into a blender.
2. Blend on high until smooth and creamy.
3. Taste and adjust the sweetness if necessary, by adding more honey.
4. Pour the smoothie into a glass and enjoy immediately for a refreshing and energizing start to your day.

NUTRITIONAL VALUES (APPROXIMATE):

Calories: 300 kcal; **Carbohydrates:** 40 g; **Proteins:** 25 g; **Fats:** 5 g; **Cholesterol:** 0 mg; **Sodium:** 150 mg; **Fiber:** 4 g.

CHAPTER 10
LUNCH

Pasta and Grains

1. MEDITERRANEAN QUINOA SALAD

Introduction:
Embrace the vibrant flavors of the Mediterranean with this nutritious and delicious Mediterranean Quinoa Salad. Packed with protein-rich quinoa, juicy cherry tomatoes, crisp cucumbers, and tangy Kalamata olives, this salad is tossed with crumbled low-fat feta cheese and dressed in a simple olive oil and lemon juice vinaigrette. It's a perfect dish for a refreshing lunch that's both satisfying and healthy.

PREPARATION TIME: 15 MINUTES
COOKING TIME: 15 MINUTES (FOR QUINOA)
TOTAL TIME: 30 MINUTES
DIFFICULTY: EASY
SERVINGS: 4

PROCEDURE:

1. In a medium saucepan, combine quinoa and water. Bring to a boil, then reduce heat to low, cover, and simmer for about 15 minutes, or until the quinoa is tender and the water is absorbed. Fluff with a fork and let cool.
2. In a large bowl, combine the cooled quinoa, cherry tomatoes, cucumber, Kalamata olives, and red onion.
3. In a small bowl, whisk together the olive oil, lemon juice, salt, and pepper to create the dressing.
4. Pour the dressing over the quinoa mixture and toss to coat evenly.
5. Gently fold in the crumbled feta cheese.
6. Serve the salad at room temperature or chilled, adjusting seasoning with salt and pepper as needed.

INGREDIENTS:

- 1 cup quinoa, rinsed
- 2 cups water
- 1 cup cherry tomatoes, halved
- 1 cucumber, diced
- ½ cup Kalamata olives, pitted and halved
- ½ red onion, finely chopped
- ¾ cup low-fat feta cheese, crumbled
- 3 tablespoons extra virgin olive oil
- Juice of 1 lemon
- Salt and pepper, to taste

NUTRITIONAL VALUES (APPROXIMATE, PER SERVING):
Calories: 350 kcal; **Carbohydrates:** 40 g; **Proteins:** 12 g; **Fats:** 18 g; **Fiber:** 5 g.

2. WHOLE WHEAT SPRING PASTA

Introduction:

Celebrate the flavors of spring with this Whole Wheat Spring Pasta, a light yet satisfying dish that showcases the best of seasonal produce. Whole wheat pasta provides a nutritious base, combined with tender asparagus, sweet peas, and zucchini, all tossed in a light basil pesto and sprinkled with grated Parmesan cheese. It's a delightful meal that brings freshness and taste to your lunchtime.

PREPARATION TIME: 10 MINUTES
COOKING TIME: 15 MINUTES
TOTAL TIME: 25 MINUTES
DIFFICULTY: EASY
SERVINGS: 4

INGREDIENTS:

- 8 ounces whole wheat pasta
- 1 cup asparagus, trimmed and cut into 1-inch pieces
- 1 cup peas (fresh or frozen)
- 1 medium zucchini, sliced
- ¼ cup light basil pesto
- ¼ cup grated Parmesan cheese
- Salt and pepper, to taste

PROCEDURE:

1. Cook the whole wheat pasta in a large pot of boiling salted water according to package instructions until al dente. In the last 3 minutes of cooking, add the asparagus and peas to blanch. Drain well and return to the pot.
2. While the pasta cooks, lightly sauté the sliced zucchini in a pan over medium heat until just tender, about 3-4 minutes. Season with a little salt and pepper.
3. Add the cooked zucchini and light basil pesto to the pasta and vegetables. Toss everything together until the pasta and vegetables are evenly coated with pesto.
4. Serve the pasta warm, sprinkled with grated Parmesan cheese on top.

NUTRITIONAL VALUES (APPROXIMATE, PER SERVING):

Calories: 320 kcal; **Carbohydrates:** 55 g; **Proteins:** 12 g; **Fats:** 7 g; **Fiber:** 8 g.

3. FARRO WITH ROASTED VEGETABLES

Introduction:

Discover the hearty and earthy flavors of Farro with Roasted Vegetables, a wholesome lunch option that combines nutty farro grains with a colorful array of roasted eggplant, bell peppers, red onions, and zucchini. Drizzled with a balsamic vinegar glaze, this dish is a satisfying and nutritious meal that's as pleasing to the palate as it is to the eye.

PREPARATION TIME: 15 MINUTES
COOKING TIME: 25 MINUTES
TOTAL TIME: 40 MINUTES
DIFFICULTY: EASY
SERVINGS: 4

INGREDIENTS:

- 1 cup farro, rinsed
- 1 eggplant, cut into cubes
- 2 bell peppers (any color), cut into strips
- 1 red onion, cut into wedges
- 1 zucchini, sliced
- 3 tablespoons olive oil, divided
- 2 tablespoons balsamic vinegar
- Salt and pepper, to taste

PROCEDURE:

1. Preheat the oven to 425°F (220°C). Toss the eggplant, bell peppers, red onion, and zucchini with 2 tablespoons of olive oil, and season with salt and pepper. Spread the vegetables in a single layer on a baking sheet.
2. Roast the vegetables in the preheated oven for about 20-25 minutes, stirring once halfway through, until tender and caramelized.
3. Meanwhile, cook the farro in a pot of boiling water according to package instructions until tender. Drain and set aside.
4. In a large bowl, mix the roasted vegetables with the cooked farro. Drizzle with the remaining olive oil and balsamic vinegar and toss to combine.
5. Adjust seasoning with salt and pepper as needed and serve warm or at room temperature.

NUTRITIONAL VALUES (APPROXIMATE, PER SERVING):

Calories: 350 kcal; **Carbohydrates:** 55 g; **Proteins:** 9 g; **Fats:** 12 g; **Fiber:** 10 g.

4. BARLEY WITH CHERRY TOMATOES AND ARUGULA

Introduction:
Delve into the wholesome goodness of Barley with Cherry Tomatoes and Arugula, a light yet fulfilling dish that combines the chewy texture of barley with the juicy sweetness of cherry tomatoes and the peppery kick of arugula. Topped with shaved Parmesan cheese and toasted pine nuts and dressed with a drizzle of extra virgin olive oil, this meal is a celebration of simple, fresh flavors.

PREPARATION TIME: 10 MINUTES
COOKING TIME: 30 MINUTES
TOTAL TIME: 40 MINUTES
DIFFICULTY: EASY

SERVINGS: 4

INGREDIENTS:

- 1 cup barley, rinsed
- 2 cups water or vegetable broth
- 1 cup cherry tomatoes, halved
- 2 cups arugula
- ¼ cup shaved Parmesan cheese
- 2 tablespoons toasted pine nuts
- 3 tablespoons extra virgin olive oil
- Salt and pepper, to taste

PROCEDURE:

1. In a medium saucepan, bring the water or vegetable broth to a boil. Add the barley, reduce heat to low, cover, and simmer for about 30 minutes, or until the barley is tender and the liquid is absorbed.
2. Allow the cooked barley to cool slightly, then transfer it to a large mixing bowl.
3. Add the halved cherry tomatoes and arugula to the barley. Toss gently to combine.
4. Drizzle the salad with extra virgin olive oil, then season with salt and pepper to taste. Toss again to ensure everything is evenly coated.
5. Garnish the salad with shaved Parmesan cheese and toasted pine nuts just before serving.

NUTRITIONAL VALUES (APPROXIMATE, PER SERVING):

Calories: 350 kcal; **Carbohydrates:** 45 g; **Proteins:** 10 g; **Fats:** 16 g; **Fiber:** 9 g.

5. BULGUR, CUCUMBER, AND MINT SALAD

Introduction:
Experience the refreshing burst of flavors with this Bulgur, Cucumber, and Mint Salad, a light and nourishing dish perfect for a summer lunch. Combining the nuttiness of bulgur wheat with the crisp freshness of cucumber and the aromatic zing of fresh mint, this salad is tossed in a zesty lemon and olive oil dressing, making it a delightful choice for any meal.

PREPARATION TIME: 15 MINUTES
COOKING TIME: 10 MINUTES (FOR BULGUR)
TOTAL TIME: 25 MINUTES
DIFFICULTY: EASY
SERVINGS: 4

PROCEDURE:

1. In a medium saucepan, bring the water to a boil. Add the bulgur wheat, reduce heat to low, cover, and simmer for about 10 minutes, or until the bulgur is tender and the water is absorbed.
2. Fluff the cooked bulgur with a fork and allow it to cool to room temperature.
3. In a large bowl, combine the cooled bulgur with diced cucumber, cherry tomatoes, and chopped mint.
4. In a small bowl, whisk together the lemon juice, extra virgin olive oil, salt, and pepper to create the dressing.
5. Pour the dressing over the bulgur salad and toss well to ensure even distribution of flavors.
6. Adjust the seasoning as necessary and serve the salad chilled or at room temperature.

INGREDIENTS:

- 1 cup bulgur wheat
- 2 cups water
- 1 large cucumber, diced
- 1 cup cherry tomatoes, quartered
- ¼ cup fresh mint, chopped
- Juice of 1 lemon
- 3 tablespoons extra virgin olive oil
- Salt and pepper, to taste

NUTRITIONAL VALUES (APPROXIMATE, PER SERVING):

Calories: 270 kcal; **Carbohydrates:** 40 g; **Proteins:** 6 g; **Fats:** 10 g; **Fiber:** 8 g.

White Meat

1. GRILLED CHICKEN BREAST WITH AVOCADO SALSA

Introduction:

Savor the perfect blend of flavors in this Grilled Chicken Breast with Avocado Salsa, a light yet satisfying dish that combines the juiciness of grilled chicken with the freshness of avocado salsa. Featuring ripe avocados, tomatoes, red onion, and a hint of cilantro and lime, this meal is a testament to simple ingredients creating extraordinary taste.

PREPARATION TIME: 20 MINUTES
COOKING TIME: 10 MINUTES
TOTAL TIME: 30 MINUTES
DIFFICULTY: EASY
SERVINGS: 2

INGREDIENTS FOR GRILLED CHICKEN:

- 2 lean chicken breasts
- Salt and pepper, to taste
- Olive oil

INGREDIENTS FOR AVOCADO SALSA:

- 1 ripe avocado, diced
- 1 medium tomato, diced
- ¼ red onion, finely chopped
- 2 tablespoons cilantro, chopped
- Juice of 1 lime
- Salt and pepper, to taste

PROCEDURE:

1. Preheat your grill or grill pan over medium-high heat.
2. Season the chicken breasts with salt and pepper, then lightly brush them with olive oil.
3. Grill the chicken for about 5 minutes on each side or until fully cooked through and nicely charred.
4. While the chicken is grilling, prepare the avocado salsa by combining the diced avocado, tomato, red onion, cilantro, and lime juice in a bowl. Season with salt and pepper to taste and gently mix to combine.
5. Once the chicken is cooked, let it rest for a few minutes before slicing.
6. Serve the grilled chicken topped with the fresh avocado salsa.

NUTRITIONAL VALUES (APPROXIMATE, PER SERVING):

Calories: 300 kcal; **Carbohydrates:** 15 g; **Proteins:** 35 g; **Fats:** 12 g; **Fiber:** 7 g.

2. TURKEY AND SPINACH SALAD WITH BERRY VINAIGRETTE

Introduction:

Enjoy a burst of freshness with this Turkey and Spinach Salad with Berry Vinaigrette, a delightful combination of smoked turkey breast, tender baby spinach, and an array of fresh berries. Topped with crunchy walnuts and crumbled feta cheese, and drizzled with a homemade berry vinaigrette, this salad is a flavorful and nutritious choice for any meal.

PREPARATION TIME: 15 MINUTES
COOKING TIME: 0 MINUTES
TOTAL TIME: 15 MINUTES
DIFFICULTY: EASY
SERVINGS: 2

INGREDIENTS FOR SALAD:

- 4 ounces smoked turkey breast, thinly sliced
- 4 cups baby spinach
- 1 cup mixed fresh berries (such as strawberries, blueberries, and raspberries)
- ¼ cup walnuts, toasted
- ¼ cup feta cheese, crumbled

INGREDIENTS FOR BERRY VINAIGRETTE:

- 2 tablespoons olive oil
- 1 tablespoon berry vinegar (or balsamic vinegar)
- 1 teaspoon honey
- Salt and pepper, to taste

PROCEDURE:

1. In a large salad bowl, arrange the baby spinach as the base. Top with sliced smoked turkey breast and mixed fresh berries.
2. Sprinkle toasted walnuts and crumbled feta cheese over the salad.
3. In a small bowl, whisk together the olive oil, berry vinegar, honey, salt, and pepper to create the vinaigrette.
4. Drizzle the berry vinaigrette over the salad just before serving.

NUTRITIONAL VALUES (APPROXIMATE, PER SERVING):

Calories: 350 kcal; **Carbohydrates:** 18 g; **Proteins:** 25 g; **Fats:** 22 g; **Fiber:** 4 g.

3. LEMON THYME CHICKEN WITH QUINOA

Introduction:

Lemon Thyme Chicken with Quinoa offers a delightful harmony of flavors, pairing the zestiness of lemon and the aromatic essence of thyme with the nuttiness of quinoa. Accompanied by steamed broccoli, this dish is a testament to wholesome eating, delivering a satisfying meal that's both nutritious and full of flavor.

PREPARATION TIME: 15 MINUTES

COOKING TIME: 25 MINUTES

TOTAL TIME: 40 MINUTES

DIFFICULTY: EASY

SERVINGS: 2

INGREDIENTS:

- 2 chicken breasts
- Juice and zest of 1 lemon
- 1 tablespoon fresh thyme leaves
- 1 cup quinoa, rinsed
- 2 cups water or chicken broth
- 1 cup broccoli florets, steamed
- Salt and pepper, to taste
- 2 tablespoons olive oil

PROCEDURE:

1. In a small bowl, mix lemon juice, zest, thyme, salt, and pepper. Marinate the chicken breasts in this mixture for at least 15 minutes.
2. In a saucepan, bring the water or chicken broth to a boil. Add the quinoa, reduce heat to low, cover, and simmer for 15 minutes, or until all the liquid is absorbed.
3. While the quinoa is cooking, heat olive oil in a skillet over medium heat. Add the marinated chicken breasts and cook for about 6-7 minutes on each side, or until golden brown and cooked through.
4. Steam the broccoli florets until tender but still bright green, about 3-4 minutes.
5. To serve, fluff the quinoa with a fork and divide it between plates. Slice the chicken and place on top of the quinoa. Serve with steamed broccoli on the side.

NUTRITIONAL VALUES (APPROXIMATE, PER SERVING):

Calories: 550 kcal; **Carbohydrates:** 55 g; **Proteins:** 40 g; **Fats:** 20 g; **Fiber:** 8 g.

4. TURKEY AND HUMMUS WRAP

Introduction:

Enjoy a quick, nutritious, and delicious meal with the Turkey and Hummus Wrap. This wrap combines tender slices of turkey breast with creamy hummus and a colorful mix of vegetables, all wrapped up in a whole wheat tortilla. It's perfect for a light lunch or a meal on the go, providing a balanced blend of protein, fiber, and fresh flavors.

PREPARATION TIME: 10 MINUTES

COOKING TIME: 0 MINUTES

TOTAL TIME: 10 MINUTES

DIFFICULTY: EASY

SERVINGS: 2

INGREDIENTS:

- 4 whole wheat tortillas
- 8 ounces turkey breast slices
- ½ cup hummus
- 1 cup mixed vegetables (lettuce, tomatoes, cucumbers), thinly sliced
- Salt and pepper, to taste

PROCEDURE:

1. Lay out the whole wheat tortillas on a flat surface.
2. Spread each tortilla evenly with hummus.
3. Arrange the turkey breast slices and mixed vegetables on top of the hummus.
4. Season with salt and pepper to taste.
5. Carefully roll up the tortillas, folding in the sides to enclose the filling.
6. Cut each wrap in half and serve immediately.

NUTRITIONAL VALUES (APPROXIMATE, PER SERVING):

Calories: 400 kcal; **Carbohydrates:** 35 g; **Proteins:** 35 g; **Fats:** 15 g; **Fiber:** 6 g.

5. CHICKEN CAESAR SALAD WITH LIGHT DRESSING

Introduction:

Reinvent a classic with this Chicken Caesar Salad with Light Dressing, a healthier take on the beloved salad. Featuring crisp romaine lettuce, grilled chicken breast, and whole wheat croutons, all tossed with a lighter Caesar dressing and sprinkled with Parmesan cheese, this salad is both light and satisfying, perfect for a nutritious lunch.

PREPARATION TIME: 20 MINUTES
COOKING TIME: 10 MINUTES
TOTAL TIME: 30 MINUTES
DIFFICULTY: EASY
SERVINGS: 2

INGREDIENTS:

- 1 romaine lettuce heart, chopped
- 2 chicken breasts, grilled and sliced
- ½ cup whole wheat croutons
- ¼ cup light Caesar dressing
- ¼ cup Parmesan cheese, grated
- Salt and pepper, to taste

PROCEDURE:

1. Preheat the grill to medium-high heat. Season the chicken breasts with salt and pepper, and grill until cooked through, about 5 minutes per side. Let it rest for a few minutes before slicing.
2. In a large bowl, toss the chopped romaine lettuce with the light Caesar dressing until the lettuce is evenly coated.
3. Add the sliced grilled chicken and whole wheat croutons to the salad.
4. Sprinkle with grated Parmesan cheese.
5. Serve the salad immediately, offering extra light Caesar dressing on the side if desired.

NUTRITIONAL VALUES (APPROXIMATE, PER SERVING):

Calories: 350 kcal; **Carbohydrates:** 18 g; **Proteins:** 40 g; **Fats:** 14 g; **Fiber:** 3 g.

Vegetarian

1. VEGETARIAN TACOS WITH BLACK BEANS

Introduction:

Dive into the vibrant and flavorsome world of Vegetarian Tacos with Black Beans, a simple yet delicious meal that brings together the hearty texture of black beans with the fresh zest of bell peppers and onions. Served on warm corn tortillas and topped with creamy guacamole and fresh salsa, these tacos are a feast for the senses and a testament to the joy of vegetarian cooking.

PREPARATION TIME: 20 MINUTES
COOKING TIME: 10 MINUTES
TOTAL TIME: 30 MINUTES
DIFFICULTY: EASY
SERVINGS: 4

INGREDIENTS:

- 1 cup black beans, cooked and drained
- 1 bell pepper, sliced
- 1 onion, sliced
- 8 corn tortillas
- 1 cup guacamole
- 1 cup fresh salsa
- Salt and pepper, to taste
- 2 tablespoons olive oil

PROCEDURE:

1. Heat the olive oil in a skillet over medium heat. Add the sliced bell pepper and onion, seasoning with salt and pepper. Sauté until the vegetables are soft and slightly caramelized, about 5-7 minutes.
2. Stir in the black beans and cook for another 2-3 minutes, until heated through.
3. Warm the corn tortillas in a dry skillet or microwave until they are soft and pliable.
4. Assemble the tacos by spooning the black bean mixture onto each tortilla. Top with a generous dollop of guacamole and fresh salsa.
5. Serve immediately, allowing everyone to enjoy the rich blend of flavors and textures.

NUTRITIONAL VALUES (APPROXIMATE, PER SERVING):

Calories: 300 kcal; **Carbohydrates:** 40 g; **Proteins:** 10 g; **Fats:** 12 g; **Fiber:** 8 g.

2. GREEK CHICKPEA SALAD

Introduction:
Savor the fresh and tangy flavors of the Mediterranean with this Greek Chickpea Salad, a colorful and nutritious dish that combines protein-rich chickpeas with crisp tomatoes, cucumbers, and olives. Tossed with red onion and low-fat feta cheese and dressed in a simple olive oil and red wine vinegar dressing, this salad is a healthy and satisfying meal on its own or a perfect side dish for any occasion.

PREPARATION TIME: 15 MINUTES
COOKING TIME: 0 MINUTES
TOTAL TIME: 15 MINUTES
DIFFICULTY: EASY
SERVINGS: 4

INGREDIENTS:

- 2 cups chickpeas, cooked and drained
- 1 cup tomatoes, diced
- 1 cup cucumbers, diced
- ½ cup olives, halved
- ¼ cup red onion, thinly sliced
- ¾ cup low-fat feta cheese, crumbled
- 3 tablespoons olive oil
- 1 tablespoon red wine vinegar
- Salt and pepper, to taste

PROCEDURE:

1. In a large bowl, combine the chickpeas, tomatoes, cucumbers, olives, and red onion.
2. In a small bowl, whisk together the olive oil, red wine vinegar, salt, and pepper to create the dressing.
3. Pour the dressing over the salad and toss gently to coat all the ingredients evenly.
4. Sprinkle the crumbled feta cheese over the salad just before serving.
5. Adjust the seasoning with salt and pepper as needed, and serve the salad chilled or at room temperature.

NUTRITIONAL VALUES (APPROXIMATE, PER SERVING):
Calories: 350 kcal; **Carbohydrates:** 30 g; **Proteins:** 15 g; **Fats:** 20 g; **Fiber:** 8 g.

3. QUINOA AND BLACK BEAN BURGERS

Introduction:
Delight in the wholesome goodness of Quinoa and Black Bean Burgers, a hearty vegetarian option that doesn't skimp on flavor. These burgers combine the nuttiness of quinoa with the heartiness of black beans, seasoned with a blend of spices and served on whole wheat buns for a nutritious and satisfying meal.

PREPARATION TIME: 20 MINUTES
COOKING TIME: 10 MINUTES
TOTAL TIME: 30 MINUTES
DIFFICULTY: MEDIUM
SERVINGS: 4 BURGERS

INGREDIENTS:

- 1 cup cooked quinoa
- 1 cup cooked black beans, mashed
- ½ cup whole wheat breadcrumbs
- 1 large egg, beaten
- 1 teaspoon cumin
- ½ teaspoon garlic powder
- ½ teaspoon smoked paprika
- Salt and pepper, to taste
- 4 whole wheat buns
- Toppings of choice (lettuce, tomato, onion, avocado)
- 2 tablespoons olive oil for cooking

PROCEDURE:

1. In a large bowl, combine the cooked quinoa, mashed black beans, whole wheat breadcrumbs, beaten egg, cumin, garlic powder, smoked paprika, salt, and pepper. Mix well until the ingredients are evenly distributed.
2. Divide the mixture into four equal portions and shape each into a burger patty.
3. Heat the olive oil in a skillet over medium heat. Cook the patties for about 5 minutes on each side, or until they are golden brown and cooked through.
4. Serve the burgers on whole wheat buns, topped with your choice of lettuce, tomato, onion, and avocado.

NUTRITIONAL VALUES (APPROXIMATE, PER BURGER):
Calories: 350 kcal; **Carbohydrates:** 45 g; **Proteins:** 15 g; **Fats:** 12 g; **Fiber:** 10 g.

4. LENTIL AND VEGETABLE CASSEROLE

Introduction:
Warm up with this comforting Lentil and Vegetable Casserole, a rich and flavorful dish that's perfect for any season. Packed with lentils, carrots, celery, and tomatoes, and seasoned with a blend of herbs, this casserole is a nourishing meal that's both satisfying and healthy.

PREPARATION TIME: 15 MINUTES
COOKING TIME: 45 MINUTES
TOTAL TIME: 1 HOUR
DIFFICULTY: MEDIUM
SERVINGS: 4

PROCEDURE:
1. Preheat your oven to 375°F (190°C).
2. In a large oven-safe pot or Dutch oven, heat a drizzle of olive oil over medium heat. Add the garlic, carrots, and celery, sautéing until softened, about 5 minutes.
3. Add the lentils, diced tomatoes (with their juice), thyme, oregano, and vegetable broth. Stir to combine and bring the mixture to a boil.
4. Cover the pot with a lid or foil and transfer it to the preheated oven.
5. Bake for about 45 minutes, or until the lentils are tender and the liquid has been absorbed.
6. Season with salt and pepper to taste before serving.

INGREDIENTS:
- 1 cup lentils, rinsed
- 2 carrots, diced
- 2 stalks celery, diced
- 1 can diced tomatoes (14 oz)
- 2 cloves garlic, minced
- 1 teaspoon dried thyme
- 1 teaspoon dried oregano
- 4 cups low-sodium vegetable broth
- Salt and pepper, to taste
- Olive oil

NUTRITIONAL VALUES (APPROXIMATE, PER SERVING):
Calories: 250 kcal; **Carbohydrates:** 40 g; **Proteins:** 15 g; **Fats:** 4 g; **Fiber:** 15 g.

5. CAULIFLOWER CRUST PIZZA

Introduction:
Indulge in a lighter version of a classic favorite with this Cauliflower Crust Pizza. Topped with tomato sauce, low-fat mozzarella, and an array of colorful vegetables, this pizza offers all the flavors you love with a nutritious twist. It's a delicious and guilt-free option that's sure to satisfy your pizza cravings.

PREPARATION TIME: 20 MINUTES
COOKING TIME: 30 MINUTES
TOTAL TIME: 50 MINUTES
DIFFICULTY: MEDIUM
SERVINGS: 2

PROCEDURE:
1. Preheat your oven to 400°F (200°C) and line a baking sheet with parchment paper.
2. In a bowl, combine the riced cauliflower, beaten egg, ½ cup of mozzarella cheese, oregano, salt, and pepper. Mix well until a dough-like consistency is formed.
3. Press the cauliflower mixture onto the parchment paper, shaping it into a pizza base.
4. Bake the crust for 20 minutes, or until it's golden and firm.
5. Remove the crust from the oven and spread tomato sauce over the top. Add your choice of vegetable toppings and sprinkle with additional mozzarella cheese.
6. Return the pizza to the oven and bake for an additional 10 minutes, or until the cheese is melted and bubbly.
7. Serve hot, cutting the pizza into slices.

INGREDIENTS:
- 1 large head of cauliflower, rice and drained
- 1 egg, beaten
- ½ cup low-fat mozzarella cheese, shredded (plus extra for topping)
- 1 teaspoon dried oregano
- Salt and pepper, to taste
- ½ cup tomato sauce
- Assorted vegetables (such as bell peppers, onions, mushrooms) for topping

NUTRITIONAL VALUES (APPROXIMATE, PER SERVING):
Calories: 300 kcal; **Carbohydrates:** 25 g; **Proteins:** 20 g; **Fats:** 15 g; **Fiber:** 8 g.

Pescetarian

1. BAKED SALMON WITH AVOCADO SAUCE

Introduction:
Experience the harmonious blend of flavors in this Baked Salmon with Avocado Sauce, a dish that pairs the rich, buttery texture of perfectly baked salmon with a creamy and zesty avocado sauce.

PREPARATION TIME: 15 MINUTES
COOKING TIME: 20 MINUTES
TOTAL TIME: 35 MINUTES
DIFFICULTY: EASY
SERVINGS: 2

PROCEDURE:
1. Preheat your oven to 400°F (200°C). Line a baking sheet with parchment paper.
2. Season the salmon fillets with salt and pepper, then drizzle with olive oil. Place the salmon on the prepared baking sheet.
3. Bake the salmon in the preheated oven for about 15-20 minutes, or until it flakes easily with a fork.
4. While the salmon is baking, prepare the avocado sauce. In a blender or food processor, combine the ripe avocado, lemon juice, minced garlic, salt, and pepper. Blend until smooth, adding a little water if necessary to achieve a creamy consistency.
5. Once the salmon is done, let it rest for a couple of minutes.
6. Serve the baked salmon drizzled with the avocado sauce and garnished with chopped chives.

INGREDIENTS FOR SALMON:
- 2 salmon fillets (about 6 ounces each)
- Salt and pepper, to taste
- 1 tablespoon olive oil

INGREDIENTS FOR AVOCADO SAUCE:
- 1 ripe avocado
- Juice of 1 lemon
- 1 clove garlic, minced
- 2 tablespoons chives, chopped
- Salt and pepper, to taste
- Water (as needed for consistency)

NUTRITIONAL VALUES (APPROXIMATE, PER SERVING):
Calories: 450 kcal; **Carbohydrates:** 10 g; **Proteins:** 35 g; **Fats:** 30 g; **Fiber:** 7 g.

2. FRESH TUNA SALAD WITH EDAMAME AND AVOCADO

Introduction:
Delight in the fresh and vibrant flavors of this Fresh Tuna Salad with Edamame and Avocado, a dish that combines succulent fresh tuna with the crunch of edamame and the creaminess of avocado.

PREPARATION TIME: 20 MINUTES
COOKING TIME: 0 MINUTES
TOTAL TIME: 20 MINUTES
DIFFICULTY: EASY
SERVINGS: 2

PROCEDURE:
1. In a large bowl, combine the diced fresh tuna, cooked edamame, and diced avocado.
2. Sprinkle the sesame seeds over the salad.
3. In a small bowl, whisk together the low-sodium soy sauce and sesame oil. Drizzle this dressing over the salad, tossing gently to coat all the ingredients evenly.
4. Season with salt and pepper to taste.
5. Serve the salad immediately, offering a fresh and satisfying meal that's as pleasing to the eye as it is to the palate.

INGREDIENTS:
- 8 ounces fresh tuna, diced
- 1 cup edamame, shelled and cooked
- 1 ripe avocado, diced
- 1 tablespoon sesame seeds
- 2 tablespoons low-sodium soy sauce
- 1 teaspoon sesame oil
- Salt and pepper, to taste

NUTRITIONAL VALUES (APPROXIMATE, PER SERVING):
Calories: 400 kcal; **Carbohydrates:** 15 g; **Proteins:** 35 g; **Fats:** 22 g; **Fiber:** 7 g.

3. SHRIMP TACOS WITH SPICY COLESLAW

Introduction:

Inject a burst of flavor into your lunchtime with Shrimp Tacos with Spicy Coleslaw. This dish features succulent shrimp paired with a tangy and spicy coleslaw, all nestled in soft corn tortillas. Topped with a squeeze of fresh lime and spicy salsa, these tacos offer a delightful combination of textures and flavors that are sure to please.

PREPARATION TIME: 20 MINUTES

COOKING TIME: 10 MINUTES

TOTAL TIME: 30 MINUTES

DIFFICULTY: EASY

SERVINGS: 4

INGREDIENTS:

- 1 lb shrimp, peeled and deveined
- 2 cups red cabbage, shredded
- 1 carrot, shredded
- 1/4 cup lime juice
- 8 corn tortillas
- 1/2 cup spicy salsa
- Salt and pepper, to taste
- 1 tablespoon olive oil
- For the Coleslaw Dressing:
- 3 tablespoons mayonnaise
- 1 tablespoon apple cider vinegar
- 1 teaspoon honey
- 1/2 teaspoon chili flakes (adjust to taste)
- Salt and pepper, to taste

PROCEDURE:

1. In a large bowl, mix together the mayonnaise, apple cider vinegar, honey, chili flakes, salt, and pepper to make the coleslaw dressing.
2. Add the shredded cabbage and carrot to the bowl with the dressing and toss until well coated. Set aside to let the flavors meld.
3. Heat the olive oil in a pan over medium heat. Season the shrimp with salt and pepper, then cook until pink and opaque, about 2-3 minutes per side.
4. Warm the corn tortillas in a dry skillet or microwave until soft and pliable.
5. Assemble the tacos by placing a portion of the shrimp on each tortilla, followed by a generous helping of the spicy coleslaw.
6. Top each taco with spicy salsa and a squeeze of lime juice before serving.

NUTRITIONAL VALUES (APPROXIMATE, PER SERVING):

Calories: 350 kcal; **Carbohydrates:** 35 g; **Proteins:** 25 g; **Fats:** 12 g; **Fiber:** 5 g.

4. WHOLE WHEAT SQUID INK SPAGHETTI WITH SEAFOOD

Introduction:

Dive into the deep flavors of the ocean with Whole Wheat Squid Ink Spaghetti with Seafood, a visually striking and deliciously rich dish. Combining the unique taste of squid ink pasta with a medley of mixed seafood, garlic, chili flakes, and cherry tomatoes, this dish is finished with a sprinkle of fresh parsley for a gourmet meal that's surprisingly easy to prepare.

PREPARATION TIME: 15 MINUTES

COOKING TIME: 20 MINUTES

TOTAL TIME: 35 MINUTES

DIFFICULTY: MEDIUM

SERVINGS: 4

INGREDIENTS:

- 8 ounces whole wheat squid ink spaghetti
- 1 lb mixed seafood (such as shrimp, scallops, and calamari rings)
- 2 cloves garlic, minced
- 1/2 teaspoon chili flakes
- 1 cup cherry tomatoes, halved
- 1/4 cup parsley, chopped
- 2 tablespoons olive oil
- Salt and pepper, to taste

PROCEDURE:

1. Cook the squid ink spaghetti according to package instructions until al dente. Drain and set aside.
2. Heat the olive oil in a large pan over medium heat. Add the minced garlic and chili flakes, cooking until fragrant.
3. Add the mixed seafood to the pan, seasoning with salt and pepper. Cook until the seafood is just done, about 5-7 minutes.
4. Stir in the cherry tomatoes and cook for another 2 minutes, until they start to soften.
5. Toss the cooked spaghetti with the seafood mixture in the pan, ensuring the pasta is well coated with the sauce and ingredients.
6. Sprinkle with chopped parsley before serving.

NUTRITIONAL VALUES (APPROXIMATE, PER SERVING):

Calories: 400 kcal; **Carbohydrates:** 50 g; **Proteins:** 30 g; **Fats:** 10 g; **Fiber:** 6 g.

5. SARDINE BRUSCHETTA ON WHOLE WHEAT BREAD

Introduction:

Enjoy the rustic simplicity of Sardine Bruschetta on Whole Wheat Bread, a nutritious and flavorful dish that highlights the natural taste of sardines. Paired with the freshness of tomato and basil on toasted whole wheat bread, this bruschetta offers a healthy twist on a classic appetizer or a light lunch option.

PREPARATION TIME: 10 MINUTES
COOKING TIME: 5 MINUTES
TOTAL TIME: 15 MINUTES
DIFFICULTY: EASY
SERVINGS: 4

INGREDIENTS:

- 4 slices of whole wheat bread, toasted
- 2 cans of sardines in olive oil, drained
- 1 tomato, finely chopped
- 1/4 cup basil leaves, chopped
- 1 clove garlic, halved
- Salt and pepper, to taste
- Extra virgin olive oil, for drizzling

PROCEDURE:

1. Rub the halved garlic clove over the surface of each slice of toasted whole wheat bread for added flavor.
2. Top each slice of bread with sardines, breaking them up slightly with a fork if desired.
3. Sprinkle the chopped tomato and basil over the sardines. Season with salt and pepper to taste.
4. Drizzle a little extra virgin olive oil over each bruschetta before serving.

NUTRITIONAL VALUES (APPROXIMATE, PER SERVING):

Calories: 250 kcal; **Carbohydrates:** 20 g; **Proteins:** 15 g; **Fats:** 12 g; **Fiber:** 3 g.

Lean Red Meat

1. GRILLED STEAK WITH ARUGULA AND PARMESAN SALAD

Introduction:

Savor the rich, bold flavors of Grilled Steak with Arugula and Parmesan Salad, a dish that perfectly balances the juiciness of grilled lean steak with the peppery bite of arugula and the salty tang of shaved Parmesan. Dressed in a simple olive oil and lemon juice vinaigrette, this meal is a testament to the power of quality ingredients coming together in harmony.

PREPARATION TIME: 15 MINUTES
COOKING TIME: 10 MINUTES
TOTAL TIME: 25 MINUTES
DIFFICULTY: EASY
SERVINGS: 2

INGREDIENTS:

- 2 lean steaks (such as sirloin or filet mignon), about 6 ounces each
- 4 cups arugula
- ¼ cup shaved Parmesan cheese
- 2 tablespoons extra virgin olive oil
- Juice of 1 lemon
- Salt and pepper, to taste

PROCEDURE:

1. Preheat your grill to medium-high heat. Season the steaks with salt and pepper.
2. Grill the steaks to your preferred doneness, about 4-5 minutes per side for medium-rare, depending on thickness. Let them rest for a few minutes before slicing thinly against the grain.
3. In a large bowl, toss the arugula with olive oil, lemon juice, salt, and pepper.
4. Divide the arugula salad among plates. Top with sliced steak and shaved Parmesan cheese.
5. Serve immediately, enjoying the melding of flavors in each bite.

NUTRITIONAL VALUES (APPROXIMATE, PER SERVING):

Calories: 450 kcal; **Carbohydrates:** 3 g; **Proteins:** 40 g; **Fats:** 30 g; **Fiber:** 1 g.

2. ROSEMARY BEEF TENDERLOIN WITH STEAMED VEGETABLES

Introduction:

Indulge in the elegance of Rosemary Beef Tenderloin with Steamed Vegetables, a dish that showcases the tenderness of beef tenderloin infused with the aromatic flavor of fresh rosemary and garlic.

PREPARATION TIME: 20 MINUTES
COOKING TIME: 30 MINUTES
TOTAL TIME: 50 MINUTES
DIFFICULTY: MEDIUM
SERVINGS: 2

PROCEDURE:

1. Preheat your oven to 400°F (200°C).
2. Rub the beef tenderloin with olive oil, then season with rosemary, garlic, salt, and pepper.
3. Place the tenderloin in a roasting pan and roast in the preheated oven until the meat reaches your desired level of doneness, about 25-30 minutes for medium-rare.
4. While the beef is roasting, steam the mixed vegetables until tender but still crisp, about 5-7 minutes.
5. Let the beef rest for 10 minutes after removing it from the oven, then slice thinly.
6. Serve the sliced beef tenderloin alongside the steamed vegetables.

INGREDIENTS:

- 1 pound lean beef tenderloin
- 2 tablespoons fresh rosemary, finely chopped
- 2 cloves garlic, minced
- 2 cups mixed vegetables (carrots, broccoli, zucchini), cut into bite-sized pieces
- 2 tablespoons extra virgin olive oil
- Salt and pepper, to taste

NUTRITIONAL VALUES (APPROXIMATE, PER SERVING):

Calories: 500 kcal; **Carbohydrates:** 10 g; **Proteins:** 45 g; **Fats:** 30 g; **Fiber:** 3 g.

3. LEAN BEEF CHILI WITH BEANS

Introduction:

Warm up with a bowl of Lean Beef Chili with Beans, a hearty and flavorful dish that combines lean beef with the rich textures of black beans and a medley of vegetables. Infused with a blend of chili spices, this chili is not only satisfying but also packed with protein and fiber, making it a perfect meal for colder days or whenever you need a comforting boost.

PREPARATION TIME: 15 MINUTES
COOKING TIME: 1 HOUR
TOTAL TIME: 1 HOUR 15 MINUTES
DIFFICULTY: EASY
SERVINGS: 4

INGREDIENTS:

- 1-pound lean beef, ground
- 1 can black beans (15 oz), drained and rinsed
- 1 can tomatoes (14 oz), diced
- 1 bell pepper, diced
- 1 onion, diced
- 2 cloves garlic, minced
- 2 tablespoons chili powder
- 1 teaspoon cumin
- 1 teaspoon smoked paprika
- 2 cups low-sodium beef broth
- Salt and pepper, to taste
- Olive oil for cooking

PROCEDURE:

1. Heat a large pot over medium heat and add a drizzle of olive oil. Cook the onion, bell pepper, and garlic until softened, about 5 minutes.
2. Add the ground lean beef to the pot, breaking it apart with a spoon. Cook until browned, about 8-10 minutes.
3. Stir in the chili powder, cumin, and smoked paprika, cooking for another minute until fragrant.
4. Add the diced tomatoes (with their juice), black beans, and beef broth. Season with salt and pepper.
5. Bring the mixture to a simmer, then reduce the heat to low. Cover and let it simmer for at least 1 hour, stirring occasionally. For a thicker chili, leave the pot uncovered for the last 15-20 minutes.
6. Serve the chili hot, garnished with your choice of toppings such as shredded cheese, sour cream, or green onions.

NUTRITIONAL VALUES (APPROXIMATE, PER SERVING):

Calories: 350 kcal; **Carbohydrates:** 30 g; **Proteins:** 35 g; **Fats:** 10 g; **Fiber:** 8 g.

4. THAI BEEF SALAD

Introduction:

Experience the fresh and tangy flavors of Thai cuisine with this Thai Beef Salad, a light yet satisfying dish. Grilled lean beef is tossed with a mix of lettuce, cucumbers, cilantro, and mint, dressed in a spicy lime and fish sauce vinaigrette.

PREPARATION TIME: 20 MINUTES
COOKING TIME: 10 MINUTES
TOTAL TIME: 30 MINUTES
DIFFICULTY: EASY
SERVINGS: 2

INGREDIENTS:

- 1-pound lean beef (such as sirloin), grilled and thinly sliced
- 4 cups mixed lettuce leaves
- 1 cucumber, thinly sliced
- ½ cup fresh cilantro leaves
- ½ cup fresh mint leaves
- 1 small chili, thinly sliced
- Juice of 2 limes
- 2 tablespoons fish sauce
- 1 teaspoon sugar
- Salt, to taste

PROCEDURE:

1. In a small bowl, whisk together the lime juice, fish sauce, sugar, and salt to create the dressing. Adjust the seasoning according to taste.
2. In a large salad bowl, combine the mixed lettuce, cucumber slices, cilantro leaves, mint leaves, and sliced chili.
3. Add the grilled and sliced lean beef to the salad.
4. Drizzle the dressing over the salad and toss gently to combine all the ingredients well.
5. Serve the salad immediately, ensuring a vibrant mix of flavors in every bite.

NUTRITIONAL VALUES (APPROXIMATE, PER SERVING):

Calories: 400 kcal; **Carbohydrates:** 15 g; **Proteins:** 50 g; **Fats:** 15 g; **Fiber:** 2 g.

5. BEEF TARTARE WITH AVOCADO

Introduction:

Indulge in the luxurious simplicity of Beef Tartare with Avocado, a refined dish that pairs the delicate taste of lean beef tenderloin with the creamy richness of avocado. Enhanced with the sharpness of red onion, the tang of capers, and a squeeze of lemon, this dish is a celebration of high-quality ingredients and sophisticated flavors, perfect for a special lunch or appetizer.

PREPARATION TIME: 20 MINUTES
TOTAL TIME: 20 MINUTES
DIFFICULTY: ADVANCED
SERVINGS: 2

INGREDIENTS:

- 8 ounces lean beef tenderloin, very finely chopped
- 1 ripe avocado, diced
- 2 tablespoons red onion, finely chopped
- 1 tablespoon capers, rinsed and chopped
- Juice of 1 lemon
- 2 tablespoons extra virgin olive oil
- Salt and pepper, to taste

PROCEDURE:

1. In a medium bowl, combine the finely chopped beef tenderloin with the diced avocado, red onion, and capers.
2. In a small bowl, whisk together the lemon juice, extra virgin olive oil, salt, and pepper.
3. Pour the dressing over the beef and avocado mixture, gently tossing to ensure everything is evenly coated.
4. Season with additional salt and pepper to taste.
5. Divide the tartare between plates, shaping them into neat rounds using a ring mold if desired.
6. Serve immediately, accompanied by toasted whole wheat bread or crackers.

NUTRITIONAL VALUES (APPROXIMATE, PER SERVING):

Calories: 450 kcal; **Carbohydrates:** 10 g; **Proteins:** 30 g; **Fats:** 32 g; **Fiber:** 5 g.

CHAPTER 11
SNACKS

1. CARROT STICKS AND HUMMUS

Introduction:
Enjoy a healthy and refreshing snack with Carrot Sticks and Hummus. This simple yet delightful combination pairs the natural sweetness and crunch of fresh carrot sticks with the creamy, savory flavor of homemade hummus. It's a perfect snack for any time of day that's not only delicious but also packed with nutrients.

PREPARATION TIME: 15 MINUTES
COOKING TIME: 0 MINUTES
TOTAL TIME: 15 MINUTES
DIFFICULTY: EASY
SERVINGS: 1

INGREDIENTS FOR CARROT STICKS:

- 2 large carrots, peeled and cut into sticks

INGREDIENTS FOR HUMMUS:

- ½ cup cooked chickpeas
- 1 tablespoon tahini
- 1 tablespoon lemon juice
- 1 clove garlic, minced
- 2 tablespoons olive oil
- Salt and pepper, to taste

PROCEDURE:

1. To make the hummus, blend the chickpeas, tahini, lemon juice, garlic, olive oil, salt, and pepper in a food processor until smooth. If the mixture is too thick, add a little water to reach the desired consistency.
2. Chill the hummus in the refrigerator for at least 30 minutes before serving to enhance its flavors.
3. Serve the hummus with the fresh carrot sticks for dipping.

NUTRITIONAL VALUES (APPROXIMATE):
Calories: 250 kcal; **Carbohydrates:** 20 g; **Proteins:** 6 g; **Fats:** 18 g; **Fiber:** 5 g.

2. OAT AND BANANA MUFFINS

Introduction:
These Oat and Banana Muffins are the perfect healthy treat to satisfy your sweet tooth without the guilt. Made with whole oats, ripe bananas, and a touch of honey, these muffins are moist, flavorful, and naturally sweetened. They're ideal for a quick breakfast, a snack, or a healthy dessert.

PREPARATION TIME: 10 MINUTES
COOKING TIME: 20 MINUTES
TOTAL TIME: 30 MINUTES
DIFFICULTY: EASY
SERVINGS: 6 MUFFINS

INGREDIENTS:

- 1 cup whole oats
- 2 ripe bananas, mashed
- 2 eggs
- ¼ cup honey
- 1 teaspoon cinnamon
- 1 teaspoon baking powder
- Olive oil or non-stick spray for greasing

PROCEDURE:

1. Preheat your oven to 350°F (175°C) and grease a muffin tin with olive oil or non-stick spray.
2. In a large bowl, mix together the mashed bananas, eggs, and honey.
3. Add the whole oats, cinnamon, and baking powder to the wet ingredients and stir until just combined.
4. Divide the batter evenly among the muffin tin cups.
5. Bake in the preheated oven for 20 minutes, or until a toothpick inserted into the center of a muffin comes out clean.
6. Allow the muffins to cool before serving.

NUTRITIONAL VALUES (APPROXIMATE, PER MUFFIN):
Calories: 150 kcal; **Carbohydrates:** 25 g; **Proteins:** 4 g; **Fats:** 4 g; **Fiber:** 3 g.

3. SPICED TOASTED NUTS

Introduction:
Indulge in the warm, spicy flavors of Spiced Toasted Nuts, a delightful snack that combines the natural richness of mixed nuts with a savory blend of spices. This easy-to-make snack is perfect for curbing hunger pangs or serving at gatherings, providing a healthy dose of proteins and healthy fats.

PREPARATION TIME: 5 MINUTES
COOKING TIME: 10 MINUTES
TOTAL TIME: 15 MINUTES
DIFFICULTY: EASY
SERVINGS: 4

INGREDIENTS:

- 1 cup mixed nuts (such as almonds, walnuts, and pecans)
- 1 egg white
- ½ teaspoon cinnamon
- ½ teaspoon paprika
- ¼ teaspoon black pepper
- A pinch of sea salt

PROCEDURE:

1. Preheat your oven to 350°F (175°C) and line a baking sheet with parchment paper.
2. In a bowl, lightly beat the egg white until frothy.
3. Add the mixed nuts to the bowl and toss until well coated with the egg white.
4. Sprinkle the cinnamon, paprika, black pepper, and sea salt over the nuts and toss again to evenly distribute the spices.
5. Spread the nuts in a single layer on the prepared baking sheet.
6. Bake in the preheated oven for 10 minutes, or until the nuts are toasted and fragrant.
7. Let the nuts cool before serving. They will become crunchier as they cool.

NUTRITIONAL VALUES (APPROXIMATE, PER SERVING):
Calories: 200 kcal; **Carbohydrates:** 9 g; **Proteins:** 6 g; **Fats:** 17 g; **Fiber:** 3 g.

4. STEAMED EDAMAME WITH SEA SALT

Introduction:
Steamed Edamame with Sea Salt is a simple, nutritious snack that's popular in Japanese cuisine. These young soybeans are steamed until tender and then sprinkled with sea salt, offering a perfect balance of taste and health benefits. Enjoy them as a snack or appetizer that's rich in protein and fiber.

PREPARATION TIME: 2 MINUTES
COOKING TIME: 5 MINUTES
TOTAL TIME: 7 MINUTES
DIFFICULTY: EASY
SERVINGS: 2

INGREDIENTS:

- 1 cup edamame, still in the pods
- 1 teaspoon sea salt
- Optional: chili flakes for a spicy kick

PROCEDURE:

1. Bring a pot of water to a boil. Add the edamame and cook for about 5 minutes, or until tender.
2. Drain the edamame and transfer to a bowl.
3. Sprinkle with sea salt, and add chili flakes if using, tossing to coat evenly.
4. Serve warm or at room temperature, enjoying the edamame by popping the beans out of the pods directly into your mouth.

NUTRITIONAL VALUES (APPROXIMATE, PER SERVING):
Calories: 100 kcal; **Carbohydrates:** 9 g; **Proteins:** 8 g; **Fats:** 4 g; **Fiber:** 4 g.

5. HOMEMADE ENERGY BARS

Introduction:
Power through your day with these nutrient-packed Homemade Energy Bars. Made with dates, nuts, and seeds, these bars offer a perfect blend of natural sweetness and crunch, along with a boost of energy. They're ideal for a quick snack, a pre-workout bite, or a convenient breakfast on the go.

PREPARATION TIME: 15 MINUTES
SETTING TIME: 1 HOUR
TOTAL TIME: 1 HOUR 15 MINUTES
DIFFICULTY: EASY
SERVINGS: 8 BARS

INGREDIENTS:
- 1 cup dates, pitted
- ½ cup almonds
- ½ cup walnuts
- 2 tablespoons chia seeds
- 2 tablespoons cocoa powder
- ¼ cup dried coconut, shredded

PROCEDURE:
1. Line an 8-inch square baking pan with parchment paper.
2. In a food processor, blend the dates, almonds, walnuts, chia seeds, and cocoa powder until the mixture sticks together and forms a sticky dough.
3. Press the mixture firmly into the prepared baking pan, creating an even layer.
4. Sprinkle the shredded coconut over the top and press lightly to adhere.
5. Chill in the refrigerator for at least 1 hour, or until firm.
6. Once set, lift the mixture out of the pan using the parchment paper and cut into 8 bars.
7. Store the energy bars in an airtight container in the refrigerator.

NUTRITIONAL VALUES (APPROXIMATE, PER BAR):
Calories: 200 kcal; **Carbohydrates:** 25 g; **Proteins:** 5 g; **Fats:** 10 g; **Fiber:** 5 g.

6. AVOCADO AND TOMATO CROSTINI

Introduction:
Experience the fresh and vibrant flavors of Avocado and Tomato Crostini, a delightful snack that pairs creamy avocado with juicy cherry tomatoes on top of toasted whole grain bread. It's a simple yet elegant snack that's perfect for satisfying hunger pangs or serving as an appetizer.

PREPARATION TIME: 10 MINUTES
COOKING TIME: 5 MINUTES
TOTAL TIME: 15 MINUTES
DIFFICULTY: EASY
SERVINGS: 4 CROSTINIS

INGREDIENTS:
- 4 slices whole grain bread
- 1 ripe avocado
- ½ cup cherry tomatoes, halved
- Sea salt and black pepper, to taste
- Olive oil, for drizzling

PROCEDURE:
1. Toast the whole grain bread slices until golden and crispy.
2. Mash the avocado in a bowl and season with salt and pepper.
3. Spread the mashed avocado evenly over each slice of toasted bread.
4. Top with halved cherry tomatoes and a drizzle of olive oil.
5. Season with a little more salt and pepper before serving.

NUTRITIONAL VALUES (APPROXIMATE, PER CROSTINI):
Calories: 150 kcal; **Carbohydrates:** 15 g; **Proteins:** 4 g; **Fats:** 9 g; **Fiber:** 5 g.

7. MINI VEGETABLE FRITTATAS

Introduction:
Enjoy a bite-sized burst of flavor with these Mini Vegetable Frittatas, a versatile and nutritious snack that's loaded with vegetables and protein. Perfect for a quick snack, a light breakfast, or even as a party appetizer, these frittatas are easy to make and can be customized with your favorite veggies.

PREPARATION TIME: 10 MINUTES
COOKING TIME: 20 MINUTES
TOTAL TIME: 30 MINUTES
DIFFICULTY: EASY
SERVINGS: 12 MINI FRITTATAS

PROCEDURE:
1. Preheat your oven to 350°F (175°C). Spray a 12-cup muffin tin with olive oil spray.
2. In a bowl, whisk the eggs and season with salt and pepper.
3. Stir in the chopped spinach, diced tomatoes, onions, bell peppers, and crumbled feta cheese.
4. Pour the egg mixture evenly into the prepared muffin cups, filling each about **2/3** full.
5. Bake in the preheated oven for 20 minutes, or until the frittatas are set and lightly golden on top.
6. Let them cool for a few minutes before removing from the tin. Serve warm or at room temperature.

INGREDIENTS:
- 6 eggs
- 1 cup spinach, chopped
- ½ cup tomatoes, diced
- ¼ cup onions, diced
- ¼ cup bell peppers, diced
- ¼ cup low-fat feta cheese, crumbled
- Salt and pepper, to taste
- Olive oil spray

NUTRITIONAL VALUES (APPROXIMATE, PER MINI FRITTATA):
Calories: 70 kcal; **Carbohydrates:** 2 g; **Proteins:** 5 g; **Fats:** 4 g; **Fiber:** 0.5 g.

8. BERRY AND SEED SMOOTHIE BOWL

Introduction:
Dive into the refreshing and nutritious Berry and Seed Smoothie Bowl, a vibrant blend of blueberries, raspberries, and creamy Greek yogurt, topped with a crunchy mix of chia seeds, flaxseeds, and unsweetened granola. This smoothie bowl is not just a feast for the eyes but also packs a powerful punch of antioxidants, protein, and fiber, making it an ideal snack or light meal any time of the day.

PREPARATION TIME: 10 MINUTES
COOKING TIME: 0 MINUTES
TOTAL TIME: 10 MINUTES
DIFFICULTY: EASY
SERVINGS: 1

PROCEDURE:
1. In a blender, combine the blueberries, raspberries, and Greek yogurt. Blend until smooth.
2. Pour the smoothie mixture into a bowl.
3. Top the smoothie bowl with chia seeds, flaxseeds, and unsweetened granola, creating a visually appealing pattern.
4. Serve immediately, and enjoy the delightful mix of smooth, creamy, and crunchy textures.

INGREDIENTS:
- ½ cup blueberries
- ½ cup raspberries
- ¾ cup low-fat Greek yogurt
- 1 tablespoon chia seeds
- 1 tablespoon flaxseeds
- ¼ cup unsweetened granola

NUTRITIONAL VALUES (APPROXIMATE):
Calories: 350 kcal; **Carbohydrates:** 40 g; **Proteins:** 20 g; **Fats:** 12 g; **Fiber:** 9 g.

CHAPTER 12
BEVERAGES

1. DETOX GREEN SMOOTHIE

Introduction:
Kickstart your day with this revitalizing Detox Green Smoothie, a blend of nutrient-rich ingredients designed to refresh and rejuvenate your body. Combining fresh spinach, cucumber, green apple, and ginger, with a splash of lemon juice and coconut water, this smoothie is not only delicious but also packed with vitamins, minerals, and hydration properties.

PREPARATION TIME: 5 MINUTES
COOKING TIME: 0 MINUTES
TOTAL TIME: 5 MINUTES
DIFFICULTY: EASY
SERVINGS: 1

PROCEDURE:
1. Place all ingredients in a blender.
2. Blend on high until smooth and creamy. If the smoothie is too thick, add a little more coconut water to reach your desired consistency.
3. Pour the smoothie into a glass and enjoy immediately for the best flavor and nutrient retention.

INGREDIENTS:
- 1 cup fresh spinach
- ½ cucumber, sliced
- 1 green apple, cored and sliced
- Juice of ½ lemon
- 1 cup coconut water
- 1 inch piece of fresh ginger, peeled

NUTRITIONAL VALUES (APPROXIMATE):
Calories: 120 kcal; **Carbohydrates:** 28 g; **Proteins:** 2 g; **Fats:** 0 g; **Fiber:** 5 g.

2. ANTIOXIDANT BERRY SMOOTHIE

Introduction:
Indulge in the sweet and tart flavors of this Antioxidant Berry Smoothie, a delicious blend of blueberries, strawberries, and raspberries mixed with creamy Greek yogurt and almond milk. Enriched with chia seeds for added fiber and omega-3s, this smoothie is a powerful drink to boost your daily antioxidant intake and support overall health.

PREPARATION TIME: 5 MINUTES
COOKING TIME: 0 MINUTES
TOTAL TIME: 5 MINUTES
DIFFICULTY: EASY
SERVINGS: 1

PROCEDURE:
1. Add the berries, Greek yogurt, almond milk, and chia seeds to a blender.
2. Blend on high until smooth. If the smoothie is too thick, add a little more almond milk to adjust the consistency.
3. Pour the smoothie into a glass and serve immediately, enjoying the burst of berry flavors and nutritional benefits.

INGREDIENTS:
- ½ cup blueberries
- ½ cup strawberries
- ½ cup raspberries
- ¾ cup low-fat Greek yogurt
- ½ cup almond milk
- 1 tablespoon chia seeds

NUTRITIONAL VALUES (APPROXIMATE):
Calories: 250 kcal; **Carbohydrates:** 35 g; **Proteins:** 15 g; **Fats:** 7 g; **Fiber:** 8 g.

3. COLD GREEN TEA WITH MINT AND LIME

Introduction:
Refresh and rejuvenate with a Cold Green Tea with Mint and Lime, a beverage that combines the antioxidant benefits of green tea with the coolness of mint and the zest of lime. Sweetened with a touch of honey, this drink is a perfect thirst-quencher for hot days or a refreshing pick-me-up at any time.

PREPARATION TIME: 10 MINUTES + CHILLING
COOKING TIME: 0 MINUTES
TOTAL TIME: 10 MINUTES + CHILLING
DIFFICULTY: EASY
SERVINGS: 2

PROCEDURE:
1. Brew the green tea in cold water with the tea bags and mint leaves, letting it steep in the refrigerator for at least 2 hours or overnight for a stronger flavor.
2. Remove the tea bags and mint leaves, then add lime slices to the infused tea. Sweeten with honey if desired, stirring well to combine.
3. Serve the tea over ice, garnished with additional mint leaves and lime slices for a burst of freshness.

INGREDIENTS:
- 2 green tea bags
- 4 cups cold water
- A handful of fresh mint leaves
- 1 lime, sliced
- Honey (optional, to taste)

NUTRITIONAL VALUES (APPROXIMATE, PER SERVING):
Calories: 5 kcal (without honey); **Carbohydrates:** 1 g; **Proteins:** 0 g; **Fats:** 0 g; **Fiber:** 0 g.

4. BANANA AND PEANUT BUTTER SMOOTHIE

Introduction:
Indulge in the creamy, satisfying flavors of a Banana and Peanut Butter Smoothie, a delicious blend that combines the natural sweetness of ripe bananas with the rich taste of peanut butter. Mixed with almond milk and Greek yogurt for added creaminess and protein, this smoothie is perfect as a filling breakfast or a nutritious snack.

PREPARATION TIME: 5 MINUTES
COOKING TIME: 0 MINUTES
TOTAL TIME: 5 MINUTES
DIFFICULTY: EASY
SERVINGS: 1

PROCEDURE:
1. Place the banana, peanut butter, almond milk, Greek yogurt, and ice in a blender.
2. Blend on high until smooth and creamy. If the smoothie is too thick, adjust the consistency by adding a little more almond milk.
3. Pour the smoothie into a glass and enjoy immediately, savoring the harmonious blend of flavors.

INGREDIENTS:
- 1 ripe banana
- 2 tablespoons natural unsweetened peanut butter
- ½ cup almond milk
- ½ cup low-fat Greek yogurt
- A handful of ice

NUTRITIONAL VALUES (APPROXIMATE):
Calories: 350 kcal; **Carbohydrates:** 40 g; **Proteins:** 18 g; **Fats:** 16 g; **Fiber:** 5 g.

5. GOLDEN MILK

Introduction:

Experience the warmth and healing properties of Golden Milk, a traditional Ayurvedic drink that combines the anti-inflammatory benefits of turmeric with the soothing effects of milk and spices. This comforting beverage is perfect for winding down in the evening or for an immune-boosting start to your day.

PREPARATION TIME: 5 MINUTES
COOKING TIME: 5 MINUTES
TOTAL TIME: 10 MINUTES
DIFFICULTY: EASY
SERVINGS: 1

PROCEDURE:

1. In a small saucepan, combine the milk, turmeric powder, cinnamon, black pepper, and grated ginger.
2. Heat the mixture over medium heat, stirring frequently, until it is hot but not boiling.
3. Remove from heat and strain the mixture to remove the ginger pieces.
4. Stir in the honey until dissolved.
5. Pour the golden milk into a mug and enjoy warm, embracing the comforting flavors and healthful benefits.

INGREDIENTS:

- 1 cup coconut or almond milk
- 1 teaspoon turmeric powder
- 1 tablespoon honey
- ½ teaspoon cinnamon
- A pinch of black pepper
- 1 inch piece of fresh ginger, grated

NUTRITIONAL VALUES (APPROXIMATE):

Calories: 120 kcal; **Carbohydrates:** 18 g; **Proteins:** 2 g; **Fats:** 5 g; **Fiber:** 1 g.

6. KIWI AND SPINACH SMOOTHIE

Introduction:

Refresh your senses with a Kiwi and Spinach Smoothie, a green delight that packs a punch of vitamins, minerals, and fiber. This smoothie combines the tangy taste of kiwi with nutrient-rich spinach, balanced with the sweetness of green apple and the creaminess of Greek yogurt, for a perfect drink that's both nutritious and delicious.

PREPARATION TIME: 5 MINUTES
COOKING TIME: 0 MINUTES
TOTAL TIME: 5 MINUTES
DIFFICULTY: EASY
SERVINGS: 1

PROCEDURE:

1. Place the kiwi slices, spinach, green apple, Greek yogurt, and water or almond milk in a blender.
2. Blend on high until the mixture is smooth and well combined.
3. Pour the smoothie into a glass and serve immediately, garnished with a slice of kiwi or a few spinach leaves if desired.

INGREDIENTS:

- 2 kiwis, peeled and sliced
- 1 cup fresh spinach
- 1 green apple, cored and sliced
- ½ cup low-fat Greek yogurt
- ½ cup water or almond milk

NUTRITIONAL VALUES (APPROXIMATE):

Calories: 220 kcal; **Carbohydrates:** 40 g; **Proteins:** 10 g; **Fats:** 2 g; **Fiber:** 6 g.

7. WATERMELON LIME REFRESHER

Introduction:

Cool off on a hot day with a Watermelon Lime Refresher, a hydrating and delicious beverage that combines the sweet juiciness of watermelon with the tartness of fresh lime juice. Enhanced with mint leaves and the option to add sparkling water, this drink is the epitome of summer in a glass.

PREPARATION TIME: 10 MINUTES
COOKING TIME: 0 MINUTES
TOTAL TIME: 10 MINUTES
DIFFICULTY: EASY
SERVINGS: 2

PROCEDURE:

1. In a blender, puree the watermelon cubes until smooth.
2. Strain the watermelon juice through a sieve to remove any pulp or seeds.
3. In a pitcher, combine the watermelon juice, lime juice, and mint leaves. Muddle the mint lightly to release its flavor.
4. Add ice cubes to the pitcher and top off with sparkling water if using, stirring gently to combine.
5. Serve the refresher in glasses garnished with additional mint leaves or lime wedges.

INGREDIENTS:

- 2 cups watermelon cubes
- Juice of 2 limes
- A handful of mint leaves
- Ice cubes
- Sparkling water (optional)

NUTRITIONAL VALUES (APPROXIMATE, PER SERVING):

Calories: 60 kcal; **Carbohydrates:** 15 g; **Proteins:** 1 g; **Fats:** 0 g; **Fiber:** 1 g.

8. COFFEE PROTEIN SMOOTHIE

Introduction:

Energize your morning or recover after a workout with a Coffee Protein Smoothie, a delicious blend that combines the kick of cold brew coffee with the nutritional benefits of protein powder. Mixed with almond milk, a frozen banana for creaminess, and cocoa powder for a touch of chocolate, this smoothie is a perfect on-the-go breakfast or snack.

PREPARATION TIME: 5 MINUTES
COOKING TIME: 0 MINUTES
TOTAL TIME: 5 MINUTES
DIFFICULTY: EASY
SERVINGS: 1

PROCEDURE:

1. Place the cold brew coffee, almond milk, protein powder, frozen banana, and cocoa powder in a blender.
2. Blend on high until smooth and creamy.
3. Pour the smoothie into a large glass and serve immediately, perhaps with a sprinkle of cocoa powder on top for an extra touch of flavor.

INGREDIENTS:

- 1 cup cold brew coffee
- ½ cup almond milk
- 1 scoop neutral or chocolate protein powder
- 1 frozen banana
- 1 tablespoon cocoa powder

NUTRITIONAL VALUES (APPROXIMATE):

Calories: 300 kcal; **Carbohydrates:** 35 g; **Proteins:** 25 g; **Fats:** 5 g; **Fiber:** 4 g.

CHAPTER 13
DINNER

Pasta and Grains

1. WHOLE WHEAT SPAGHETTI WITH AVOCADO PESTO

Introduction:
Dive into a heart-healthy rendition of a classic dish with Whole Wheat Spaghetti with Avocado Pesto. This recipe blends the creamy, rich flavors of avocado with the fresh zest of basil and lemon, creating a pesto sauce that's both nourishing and delicious. It's a perfect dish for those looking to enjoy traditional pasta with a healthy twist.

PREPARATION TIME: 15 MINUTES
COOKING TIME: 10 MINUTES
TOTAL TIME: 25 MINUTES
DIFFICULTY: EASY
SERVINGS: 1

PROCEDURE:
1. Cook the whole wheat spaghetti according to the package instructions until al dente. Drain and set aside.
2. In a food processor, combine the avocado, basil leaves, garlic, pine nuts, and lemon juice. Blend until smooth. Season with salt and pepper to taste.
3. Toss the cooked spaghetti with the avocado pesto until evenly coated.
4. Serve immediately, garnished with extra basil leaves or pine nuts if desired.

INGREDIENTS:
* 2 ounces whole wheat spaghetti
* 1 ripe avocado
* ¼ cup fresh basil leaves
* 1 garlic clove
* 2 tablespoons pine nuts
* 2 tablespoons lemon juice
* Salt and black pepper, to taste

NUTRITIONAL VALUES (APPROXIMATE):
Calories: 400 kcal; **Carbohydrates:** 55 g; **Proteins:** 12 g; **Fats:** 18 g; **Fiber:** 10 g.

2. BARLEY RISOTTO WITH PUMPKIN AND SAGE

Introduction:
Transform your dinner into a cozy, comforting experience with Barley Risotto with Pumpkin and Sage. This hearty dish combines the nutty flavors of barley with the sweetness of pumpkin, all infused with the aromatic essence of sage. It's a delightful twist on traditional risotto, offering a wholesome and satisfying meal perfect for chilly evenings.

PREPARATION TIME: 15 MINUTES
COOKING TIME: 45 MINUTES
TOTAL TIME: 60 MINUTES
DIFFICULTY: MEDIUM
SERVINGS: 1

INGREDIENTS:

- ½ cup barley, rinsed
- 1 cup pumpkin, diced
- 2 cups low-sodium vegetable broth, warmed
- 1 tablespoon sage, chopped
- 2 tablespoons grated Parmesan cheese
- Salt and black pepper, to taste
- 1 teaspoon olive oil

PROCEDURE:

1. Heat the olive oil in a medium saucepan over medium heat. Add the diced pumpkin and cook until it starts to soften, about 5 minutes.
2. Add the barley to the saucepan and toast for 2 minutes, stirring frequently.
3. Begin to add the warm vegetable broth, one ladle at a time, stirring occasionally. Allow the barley to absorb the broth before adding more. Continue this process until the barley is tender and creamy, about 40 minutes.
4. Stir in the chopped sage and grated Parmesan cheese. Season with salt and black pepper to taste.
5. Serve the risotto warm, garnished with additional sage or Parmesan if desired.

NUTRITIONAL VALUES (APPROXIMATE):

Calories: 350 kcal; **Carbohydrates:** 65 g; **Proteins:** 10 g; **Fats:** 5 g; **Fiber:** 15 g.

3. COUSCOUS WITH GRILLED VEGETABLES AND FETA

Introduction:
Enjoy the flavors of the Mediterranean with this Couscous with Grilled Vegetables and Feta recipe. A light yet satisfying dish, it combines fluffy whole wheat couscous with charred vegetables and the tangy bite of feta cheese. It's a perfect meal for those seeking a nutritious yet delicious option.

PREPARATION TIME: 15 MINUTES
COOKING TIME: 15 MINUTES
TOTAL TIME: 30 MINUTES
DIFFICULTY: EASY
SERVINGS: 1

PROCEDURE:

1. Prepare the couscous according to package instructions. Fluff with a fork and set aside.
2. Preheat a grill pan over medium-high heat. Toss the diced vegetables with half the olive oil and season with salt and pepper.
3. Grill the vegetables until they are tender and have grill marks, about 5-7 minutes, turning occasionally.
4. Mix the grilled vegetables with the cooked couscous. Drizzle with the remaining olive oil.
5. Top with crumbled feta cheese before serving.

INGREDIENTS:

- ½ cup whole wheat couscous
- ¼ cup eggplant, diced
- ¼ cup bell peppers, diced
- ¼ cup zucchini, diced
- 2 tablespoons low-fat feta cheese, crumbled
- 1 tablespoon olive oil
- Salt and pepper, to taste

NUTRITIONAL VALUES (APPROXIMATE):

Calories: 350 kcal; **Carbohydrates:** 50 g; **Proteins:** 12 g; **Fats:** 12 g; **Fiber:** 8 g.

4. COLD WHOLE WHEAT PASTA WITH TOMATOES, OLIVES, AND TUNA

Introduction:

This Cold Whole Wheat Pasta with Tomatoes, Olives, and Tuna is the epitome of a quick and healthy meal. Perfect for a refreshing lunch or a light dinner, it combines the hearty texture of whole wheat pasta with the robust flavors of tomatoes, olives, and tuna, all tied together with a simple olive oil and basil dressing.

PREPARATION TIME: 10 MINUTES
COOKING TIME: 10 MINUTES
TOTAL TIME: 20 MINUTES + CHILLING
DIFFICULTY: EASY
SERVINGS: 1

PROCEDURE:

1. Cook the whole wheat pasta according to the package instructions until al dente. Rinse under cold water to cool and drain well.
2. In a large bowl, combine the cooled pasta, cherry tomatoes, black olives, and tuna.
3. Drizzle with olive oil and add the torn basil leaves. Season with salt and pepper to taste.
4. Toss everything together until well mixed.
5. Chill in the refrigerator for at least 30 minutes before serving to allow the flavors to meld.

INGREDIENTS:

- 2 ounces whole wheat pasta
- ½ cup cherry tomatoes, halved
- ¼ cup black olives, sliced
- 3 ounces canned tuna in water, drained
- 2 tablespoons olive oil
- Fresh basil leaves, torn
- Salt and pepper, to taste

NUTRITIONAL VALUES (APPROXIMATE):

Calories: 400 kcal; **Carbohydrates:** 45 g; **Proteins:** 22 g; **Fats:** 18 g; **Fiber:** 6 g.

5. FARRO SALAD WITH CHICKEN, SPINACH, AND PECORINO

Introduction:

Savor the delightful combination of grains, protein, and greens in this Farro Salad with Chicken, Spinach, and Pecorino. This dish is a nutritional powerhouse, offering a balanced meal with the chewy texture of farro, the lean protein of grilled chicken, and the fresh taste of baby spinach, all beautifully complemented by the sharpness of Pecorino Romano cheese.

PREPARATION TIME: 15 MINUTES
COOKING TIME: 30 MINUTES
TOTAL TIME: 45 MINUTES
DIFFICULTY: MEDIUM
SERVINGS: 1

PROCEDURE:

1. Cook the farro according to package instructions until tender but still chewy. Drain and let cool.
2. In a large bowl, combine the cooled farro, sliced grilled chicken, baby spinach, and chopped walnuts.
3. Drizzle with olive oil and season with salt and pepper. Toss to combine.
4. Sprinkle grated Pecorino Romano cheese over the salad before serving.

INGREDIENTS:

- ½ cup farro
- 3 ounces grilled chicken breast, sliced
- 1 cup baby spinach
- 2 tablespoons Pecorino Romano cheese, grated
- 2 tablespoons walnuts, chopped
- 1 tablespoon olive oil
- Salt and pepper, to taste

NUTRITIONAL VALUES (APPROXIMATE):

Calories: 450 kcal; **Carbohydrates:** 48 g; **Proteins:** 30 g; **Fats:** 18 g; **Fiber:** 9 g.

White Meat

1. STUFFED CHICKEN BREAST WITH SPINACH AND RICOTTA

Introduction:
Elevate your dinner game with this Stuffed Chicken Breast with Ricotta, a dish that combines the tender juiciness of chicken with the creamy richness of ricotta and the nutritional punch of spinach. Drizzled with olive oil and seasoned with herbs, this recipe is both flavorful and healthy.

PREPARATION TIME: 20 MINUTES
COOKING TIME: 25 MINUTES
TOTAL TIME: 45 MINUTES
DIFFICULTY: MEDIUM
SERVINGS: 1

PROCEDURE:
1. Preheat your oven to 375°F (190°C).
2. Carefully slice the chicken breast horizontally to create a pocket, being careful not to cut all the way through.
3. In a bowl, mix the chopped spinach, ricotta cheese, herbs, salt, and pepper.
4. Stuff the mixture into the chicken breast pocket and secure it with toothpicks.
5. Heat olive oil in a skillet over medium heat and sear the chicken on both sides until golden.
6. Transfer the chicken to a baking dish and bake in the preheated oven for 20-25 minutes, or until the chicken is cooked through.
7. Remove from the oven, let rest for a few minutes, then slice and serve.

INGREDIENTS:
- 1 large chicken breast
- ½ cup fresh spinach, chopped
- ¼ cup low-fat ricotta cheese
- 1 tablespoon mixed herbs (e.g., oregano, thyme, basil)
- 1 tablespoon olive oil
- Salt and pepper, to taste

NUTRITIONAL VALUES (APPROXIMATE):
Calories: 400 kcal; **Carbohydrates:** 3 g; **Proteins:** 55 g; **Fats:** 18 g; **Fiber:** 1 g.

2. CHICKEN TAGINE WITH PRUNES AND ALMONDS

Introduction:
Dive into the exotic flavors of Morocco with this Chicken Tagine with Prunes and Almonds. This dish combines tender chicken with the sweetness of prunes and the crunch of almonds, all brought together with a fragrant blend of spices. It's a symphony of flavors that promises to transport you straight to the streets of Marrakesh.

PREPARATION TIME: 15 MINUTES
COOKING TIME: 1 HOUR
TOTAL TIME: 1 HOUR 15 MINUTES
DIFFICULTY: MEDIUM
SERVINGS: 1

PROCEDURE:
1. In a tagine or a heavy-bottomed pot, heat a drizzle of olive oil over medium heat. Add the onion and garlic, cooking until soft and fragrant.
2. Add the chicken pieces to the pot, browning them on all sides. Season with cinnamon, ginger, turmeric, salt, and pepper.
3. Add enough water to cover the chicken halfway, then add the prunes. Cover and simmer on low heat for about 45 minutes, or until the chicken is tender.
4. Uncover, increase the heat slightly, and add the toasted almonds. Cook for an additional 15 minutes, or until the sauce thickens.
5. Garnish with chopped coriander before serving.

INGREDIENTS:
- 1 chicken breast, cut into pieces
- ¼ cup dried prunes
- 2 tablespoons almonds, toasted
- ¼ onion, finely chopped
- 1 clove garlic, minced
- ¼ teaspoon cinnamon
- ¼ teaspoon ginger
- A pinch of turmeric
- 1 tablespoon coriander, chopped
- Olive oil
- Salt and pepper, to taste

NUTRITIONAL VALUES (APPROXIMATE):
Calories: 500 kcal; **Carbohydrates:** 30 g; **Proteins:** 40 g; **Fats:** 24 g; **Fiber:** 4 g.

3. BAKED TURKEY WITH HERBS AND ROOT VEGETABLES

Introduction:

Delight in the rustic charm of this Baked Turkey with Herbs and Root Vegetables, a dish that brings together the rich flavors of turkey with the earthy goodness of seasonal root vegetables, all beautifully seasoned with aromatic herbs. It's a wholesome meal that's perfect for a cozy night in.

PREPARATION TIME: 20 MINUTES
COOKING TIME: 1 HOUR 30 MINUTES
TOTAL TIME: 1 HOUR 50 MINUTES
DIFFICULTY: MEDIUM
SERVINGS: 1

INGREDIENTS:

- 8 ounces turkey breast
- ½ cup carrots, chopped
- ½ cup sweet potatoes, chopped
- ½ cup turnips, chopped
- 1 tablespoon olive oil
- 1 teaspoon fresh rosemary, chopped
- 1 teaspoon fresh thyme, chopped
- Salt and pepper, to taste

PROCEDURE:

1. Preheat your oven to 375°F (190°C).
2. In a large bowl, toss the carrots, sweet potatoes, and turnips with olive oil, rosemary, thyme, salt, and pepper until well coated.
3. Place the turkey breast in the center of a baking dish. Surround it with the seasoned root vegetables.
4. Cover the dish with aluminum foil and bake in the preheated oven for about 1 hour and 15 minutes.
5. Remove the foil, increase the oven temperature to 425°F (220°C), and continue baking for another 15 minutes, or until the vegetables are caramelized and the turkey is fully cooked.
6. Let the turkey rest for a few minutes before slicing. Serve warm with the roasted vegetables on the side.

NUTRITIONAL VALUES (APPROXIMATE):

Calories: 450 kcal; **Carbohydrates:** 40 g; **Proteins:** 50 g; **Fats:** 12 g; **Fiber:** 6 g.

4. CHICKEN AND VEGETABLE STIR-FRY WITH LIGHT SOY SAUCE

Introduction:

This Chicken and Vegetable Stir-fry with Light Soy Sauce is a quick, healthy, and delicious meal that packs a punch of flavor. It combines lean chicken breast, crisp vegetables, and a savory sauce for a dish that's both satisfying and nutritious. Perfect for a busy weeknight dinner, it's a great way to get your veggies in!

PREPARATION TIME: 10 MINUTES
COOKING TIME: 15 MINUTES
TOTAL TIME: 25 MINUTES
DIFFICULTY: EASY
SERVINGS: 1

INGREDIENTS:

- 4 ounces chicken breast, thinly sliced
- ¼ cup sliced bell peppers
- ¼ cup broccoli florets
- ¼ cup julienned carrots
- 2 tablespoons low-sodium soy sauce
- 1 teaspoon sesame oil
- 1 tablespoon olive oil
- Salt and pepper, to taste

PROCEDURE:

1. Heat the olive oil in a large skillet or wok over medium-high heat.
2. Add the chicken slices and stir-fry until they are just cooked through, about 3-5 minutes. Remove the chicken from the skillet and set aside.
3. In the same skillet, add the bell peppers, broccoli, and carrots. Stir-fry the vegetables for about 5 minutes, or until they are tender but still crisp.
4. Return the chicken to the skillet. Add the low-sodium soy sauce and sesame oil, stirring to combine all the ingredients.
5. Season with salt and pepper to taste. Cook for an additional 2-3 minutes.
6. Serve hot, straight from the skillet.

NUTRITIONAL VALUES (APPROXIMATE):

Calories: 300 kcal; **Carbohydrates:** 15 g; **Proteins:** 26 g; **Fats:** 14 g; **Fiber:** 3 g.

5. TURKEY, AVOCADO, AND TOMATO SALAD WITH LIME DRESSING

Introduction:
Light, refreshing, and brimming with flavor, this Turkey, Avocado, and Tomato Salad with Lime Dressing is the perfect dish for a health-conscious diner. Combining lean turkey with the creamy texture of avocado, the juiciness of tomatoes, and a zesty lime dressing, it's a salad that's as nutritious as it is delicious.

PREPARATION TIME: 15 MINUTES
COOKING TIME: 0 MINUTES
TOTAL TIME: 15 MINUTES
DIFFICULTY: EASY
SERVINGS: 1

PROCEDURE:

1. In a large bowl, whisk together the lime juice, olive oil, salt, and pepper to create the dressing.
2. Add the mixed lettuce leaves to the bowl and toss gently to coat with the dressing.
3. Arrange the dressed lettuce on a plate or in a bowl. Top with the sliced turkey, avocado, and cherry tomatoes.
4. Serve immediately, enjoying the fresh and vibrant flavors of this wholesome salad.

INGREDIENTS:

- 4 ounces grilled turkey breast, sliced
- ½ avocado, sliced
- ½ cup cherry tomatoes, halved
- 2 cups mixed lettuce leaves
- 1 tablespoon lime juice
- 1 tablespoon olive oil
- Salt and pepper, to taste

NUTRITIONAL VALUES (APPROXIMATE):

Calories: 350 kcal; **Carbohydrates:** 14 g; **Proteins:** 28 g; **Fats:** 22 g; **Fiber:** 7 g.

Vegetarian

1. VEGETARIAN CHILI WITH QUINOA AND BLACK BEANS

Introduction:
Savor the rich, hearty flavors of this Vegetarian Chili with Quinoa and Black Beans. Packed with protein and fiber, this chili is a wholesome blend of quinoa, black beans, and vegetables, simmered in a savory spice mix. It's perfect for a comforting meal that satisfies your taste buds and nutritional needs.

PREPARATION TIME: 15 MINUTES
COOKING TIME: 30 MINUTES
TOTAL TIME: 45 MINUTES
DIFFICULTY: EASY
SERVINGS: 1

PROCEDURE:

1. Heat the olive oil in a pot over medium heat. Add the bell peppers and sauté until soft, about 5 minutes.
2. Add the diced tomatoes, corn kernels, black beans, chili powder, cumin, and garlic powder to the pot. Stir to combine.
3. Add the cooked quinoa and 1 cup of water. Bring to a simmer, then reduce the heat and cover. Let it cook for 20 minutes, stirring occasionally.
4. Season with salt and pepper to taste. Stir in the chopped coriander just before serving.
5. Serve the chili warm, garnished with additional coriander if desired.

INGREDIENTS:

- ½ cup cooked quinoa
- ½ cup black beans, rinsed and drained
- ½ cup diced tomatoes
- ¼ cup corn kernels
- ¼ cup diced bell peppers
- 1 teaspoon chili powder
- ½ teaspoon cumin
- ¼ teaspoon garlic powder
- 2 tablespoons chopped coriander
- Salt and pepper, to taste
- 1 tablespoon olive oil

NUTRITIONAL VALUES (APPROXIMATE):

Calories: 350 kcal; **Carbohydrates:** 60 g; **Proteins:** 15 g; **Fats:** 7 g; **Fiber:** 15 g.

2. VEGETARIAN ZUCCHINI AND RICOTTA LASAGNA

Introduction:

This Vegetarian Zucchini and Ricotta Lasagna offers a light and nutritious take on the classic Italian dish. Using thinly sliced zucchini in place of traditional pasta layers, this recipe combines the creamy texture of ricotta with a flavorful tomato sauce and melted mozzarella. It's a delightful, low-carb option that doesn't compromise on taste.

PREPARATION TIME: 20 MINUTES
COOKING TIME: 40 MINUTES
TOTAL TIME: 1 HOUR
DIFFICULTY: MEDIUM
SERVINGS: 1

INGREDIENTS:

- 1 large zucchini, thinly sliced
- ½ cup low-fat ricotta cheese
- ¼ cup tomato sauce
- ¼ cup shredded light mozzarella cheese
- 1 tablespoon chopped basil
- Salt and pepper, to taste
- Olive oil spray

PROCEDURE:

1. Preheat your oven to 375°F (190°C). Spray a baking dish with olive oil spray.
2. Lay out the zucchini slices on paper towels and sprinkle lightly with salt. Let them sit for 10 minutes to draw out moisture, then pat dry.
3. In a bowl, mix the ricotta cheese with chopped basil, salt, and pepper.
4. Begin assembling the lasagna by spreading a spoonful of tomato sauce at the bottom of the baking dish.
5. Layer zucchini slices over the sauce, then spread a layer of the ricotta mixture, and sprinkle some mozzarella cheese. Repeat the layers until all ingredients are used, ending with mozzarella on top.
6. Cover with foil and bake for 30 minutes. Remove the foil and bake for another 10 minutes, or until the cheese is bubbly and golden.
7. Let it cool for a few minutes before slicing and serving.

NUTRITIONAL VALUES (APPROXIMATE):

Calories: 300 kcal; **Carbohydrates:** 20 g; **Proteins:** 25 g; **Fats:** 15 g; **Fiber:** 5 g.

3. CHICKPEA AND SPINACH CURRY

Introduction:

Indulge in the flavors of India with this vibrant Chickpea and Spinach Curry. Combining the protein-rich chickpeas with the iron-packed goodness of spinach, this dish is simmered in a fragrant curry sauce made with light coconut milk. It's a nutritious, flavorful meal that pairs perfectly with fluffy brown rice.

PREPARATION TIME: 15 MINUTES
COOKING TIME: 25 MINUTES
TOTAL TIME: 40 MINUTES
DIFFICULTY: EASY
SERVINGS: 1

INGREDIENTS:

- ½ cup cooked chickpeas
- 1 cup fresh spinach, roughly chopped
- ½ cup light coconut milk
- 1 tablespoon curry paste
- ½ cup diced tomatoes
- ¼ cup cooked brown rice
- 1 tablespoon chopped coriander
- Salt, to taste
- 1 teaspoon olive oil

PROCEDURE:

1. Heat the olive oil in a pan over medium heat. Add the curry paste and sauté for 1 minute to release the flavors.
2. Add the diced tomatoes and cook for another 5 minutes, until the tomatoes are soft, and the mixture starts to thicken.
3. Stir in the chickpeas and light coconut milk. Bring to a simmer, then reduce the heat and cook for 15 minutes, allowing the flavors to meld together.
4. Add the spinach to the pan, stirring until it wilts, about 2-3 minutes. Season with salt to taste.
5. Serve the curry over cooked brown rice, garnished with chopped coriander.

NUTRITIONAL VALUES (APPROXIMATE):

Calories: 350 kcal; **Carbohydrates:** 45 g; **Proteins:** 15 g; **Fats:** 12 g; **Fiber:** 10 g.

4. RED LENTIL BURGER WITH COLESLAW

Introduction:
Experience a delightful twist on the classic burger with this Red Lentil Burger with Coleslaw. Featuring a hearty lentil patty seasoned with spices and served on a whole wheat bun, this burger is complemented by a fresh, tangy coleslaw. It's a delicious, nutritious option for any meal.

PREPARATION TIME: 20 MINUTES
COOKING TIME: 10 MINUTES
TOTAL TIME: 30 MINUTES
DIFFICULTY: MEDIUM
SERVINGS: 1

PROCEDURE:
1. In a bowl, mash the cooked red lentils. Mix in the breadcrumbs, mixed spices, salt, and pepper until well combined.
2. Form the mixture into a patty. Heat the olive oil in a pan over medium heat and cook the patty for about 5 minutes on each side, until golden and firm.
3. In another bowl, mix the shredded cabbage and carrots with Greek yogurt, salt, and pepper to make the coleslaw.
4. Serve the lentil patty on the whole wheat bun, topped with the coleslaw.

INGREDIENTS:
- ½ cup cooked red lentils
- ¼ cup whole wheat breadcrumbs
- 1 teaspoon mixed spices (e.g., cumin, coriander, paprika)
- 1 whole wheat bun
- ½ cup shredded cabbage
- ¼ cup shredded carrots
- 2 tablespoons low-fat Greek yogurt
- Salt and pepper, to taste
- 1 teaspoon olive oil

NUTRITIONAL VALUES (APPROXIMATE):
Calories: 400 kcal; **Carbohydrates:** 60 g; **Proteins:** 20 g; **Fats:** 9 g; **Fiber:** 12 g.

5. CAULIFLOWER CRUST PIZZA WITH VEGETABLE TOPPINGS

Introduction:
Dive into a guilt-free pizza experience with this Cauliflower Crust Pizza with Vegetable Toppings. Featuring a crispy crust made from cauliflower, topped with a savory tomato sauce, light mozzarella cheese, and a colorful array of vegetables, this pizza is a delightful way to enjoy a favorite dish in a healthier way.

PREPARATION TIME: 20 MINUTES
COOKING TIME: 25 MINUTES
TOTAL TIME: 45 MINUTES
DIFFICULTY: MEDIUM
SERVINGS: 1

PROCEDURE:
1. Preheat the oven to 400°F (200°C). Line a baking sheet with parchment paper.
2. In a bowl, combine the grated cauliflower, egg, and salt. Mix well and form into a pizza base on the prepared baking sheet.
3. Bake the crust for 15-20 minutes, or until it's golden and firm.
4. Remove the crust from the oven, spread the tomato sauce over it, and sprinkle with half the mozzarella cheese.
5. Top with bell peppers, mushrooms, onions, and the rest of the mozzarella cheese. Drizzle with olive oil and season with salt and pepper.
6. Return to the oven and bake for an additional 5-10 minutes, until the cheese is melted and bubbly.
7. Serve hot, cut into slices.

INGREDIENTS:
- 1 cup grated cauliflower
- 1 egg, beaten
- ¼ cup shredded light mozzarella cheese
- ¼ cup tomato sauce
- ¼ cup bell peppers, sliced
- ¼ cup mushrooms, sliced
- ¼ cup onions, sliced
- Salt and pepper, to taste
- 1 tablespoon olive oil

NUTRITIONAL VALUES (APPROXIMATE):
Calories: 300 kcal; **Carbohydrates:** 20 g; **Proteins:** 18 g; **Fats:** 18 g; **Fiber:** 5 g.

Pescetarian

1. BAKED SEA BASS WITH OLIVES AND CHERRY TOMATOES

Introduction:
Experience the Mediterranean at your dinner table with this Baked Sea Bass with Olives and Cherry Tomatoes. This dish features succulent sea bass fillets, roasted to perfection with a vibrant mixture of cherry tomatoes, olives, and capers, all infused with the aromatic presence of garlic and thyme. It's a simple yet elegant meal that's sure to impress.

PREPARATION TIME: 10 MINUTES
COOKING TIME: 20 MINUTES
TOTAL TIME: 30 MINUTES
DIFFICULTY: EASY
SERVINGS: 1

PROCEDURE:

1. Preheat your oven to 400°F (200°C).
2. In a baking dish, place the sea bass fillet in the center. Surround it with cherry tomatoes, olives, and capers.
3. Sprinkle minced garlic and thyme over the fish and vegetables. Drizzle everything with olive oil and season with salt and pepper.
4. Bake in the preheated oven for about 20 minutes, or until the sea bass is cooked through and flakes easily with a fork.
5. Serve hot, with a drizzle of the cooking juices from the baking dish.

INGREDIENTS:

* 1 sea bass fillet
* ½ cup cherry tomatoes, halved
* ¼ cup olives, pitted
* 1 tablespoon capers
* 2 cloves garlic, minced
* 2 tablespoons olive oil
* 1 teaspoon fresh thyme leaves
* Salt and pepper, to taste

NUTRITIONAL VALUES (APPROXIMATE):
Calories: 400 kcal; **Carbohydrates:** 8 g; **Proteins:** 35 g; **Fats:** 25 g; **Fiber:** 2 g.

2. FRESH CRAB SALAD WITH AVOCADO AND MANGO

Introduction:
This Fresh Crab Salad with Avocado and Mango brings together the delicate flavors of crab meat with the creamy texture of avocado and the sweet, tropical taste of mango. Dressed in a light lemon and olive oil vinaigrette and served atop mixed greens, it's a refreshing and nutritious salad perfect for a light lunch or starter.

PREPARATION TIME: 15 MINUTES
COOKING TIME: 0 MINUTES
TOTAL TIME: 15 MINUTES
DIFFICULTY: EASY
SERVINGS: 1

PROCEDURE:

1. In a small bowl, whisk together the lemon juice, olive oil, salt, and pepper to create the dressing.
2. In a large bowl, combine the crab meat, avocado, and mango. Drizzle with the prepared dressing and toss gently to coat.
3. Place the mixed greens on a plate and top with the crab, avocado, and mango mixture.
4. Serve immediately, enjoying the harmonious blend of flavors and textures.

INGREDIENTS:

* 4 ounces crab meat, picked and cleaned
* ½ avocado, diced
* ½ mango, diced
* 2 cups mixed greens
* 1 tablespoon lemon juice
* 2 tablespoons olive oil
* Salt and pepper, to taste

NUTRITIONAL VALUES (APPROXIMATE):
Calories: 350 kcal; **Carbohydrates:** 22 g; **Proteins:** 20 g; **Fats:** 22 g; **Fiber:** 5 g.

3. GRILLED SALMON WITH YOGURT AND CUCUMBER SAUCE

Introduction:
Indulge in the rich flavors of Grilled Salmon with Yogurt and Cucumber Sauce, a dish that perfectly balances the fatty richness of salmon with the cool, tangy contrast of a Greek yogurt and cucumber sauce. Enhanced with dill and garlic, this meal is a testament to the simplicity and elegance of combining fresh ingredients.

PREPARATION TIME: 15 MINUTES
COOKING TIME: 10 MINUTES
TOTAL TIME: 25 MINUTES
DIFFICULTY: EASY
SERVINGS: 1

INGREDIENTS:
- 1 salmon fillet
- ½ cup low-fat Greek yogurt
- ½ cucumber, grated and squeezed to remove excess water
- 1 tablespoon chopped dill
- 1 clove garlic, minced
- Salt and pepper, to taste
- 1 teaspoon olive oil

PROCEDURE:
1. Preheat your grill to medium-high heat. Brush the salmon fillet with olive oil and season with salt and pepper.
2. Grill the salmon for about 5 minutes on each side, or until cooked to your liking.
3. While the salmon is grilling, prepare the sauce. In a bowl, mix together the Greek yogurt, grated cucumber, dill, minced garlic, and a pinch of salt.
4. Once the salmon is done, transfer it to a plate. Serve it with a generous dollop of the yogurt and cucumber sauce.

NUTRITIONAL VALUES (APPROXIMATE):
Calories: 450 kcal; **Carbohydrates:** 8 g; **Proteins:** 40 g; **Fats:** 28 g; **Fiber:** 1 g.

4. PASTA WITH CLAMS AND BROCCOLI

Introduction:
Dive into a sea of flavors with this Pasta with Clams and Broccoli, a dish that brings the ocean to your table. Whole wheat spaghetti serves as the perfect base for tender clams and crisp, green broccoli, all tied together with garlic, chili flakes, and a drizzle of olive oil. This recipe promises a deliciously balanced meal that's as nutritious as it is satisfying.

PREPARATION TIME: 15 MINUTES
COOKING TIME: 20 MINUTES
TOTAL TIME: 35 MINUTES
DIFFICULTY: MEDIUM
SERVINGS: 1

INGREDIENTS:
- 2 ounces whole wheat spaghetti
- ½ cup clams, cleaned
- 1 cup broccoli florets
- 2 cloves garlic, minced
- ¼ teaspoon chili flakes
- 2 tablespoons olive oil
- 2 tablespoons fresh parsley, chopped
- Salt and pepper, to taste

PROCEDURE:
1. Cook the whole wheat spaghetti according to package instructions until al dente. Drain and set aside.
2. In a large skillet, heat 1 tablespoon of olive oil over medium heat. Add the garlic and chili flakes, sautéing until fragrant, about 1 minute.
3. Add the clams to the skillet, cover, and cook until they open, about 5-7 minutes. Discard any clams that do not open.
4. In a separate pot, blanch the broccoli florets in boiling water for 2 minutes, then drain.
5. Add the cooked spaghetti and blanched broccoli to the skillet with the clams. Drizzle the remaining olive oil over the pasta and toss everything together.
6. Season with salt and pepper to taste, and garnish with chopped parsley before serving.

NUTRITIONAL VALUES (APPROXIMATE):
Calories: 400 kcal; **Carbohydrates:** 45 g; **Proteins:** 25 g; **Fats:** 15 g; **Fiber:** 6 g.

5. LIGHT SEAFOOD SOUP

Introduction:

Warm your soul with this Light Seafood Soup, a delicate broth brimming with a medley of seafood, tomatoes, and aromatic vegetables. Infused with herbs and seasoned to perfection, this soup is a light yet flavorful dish that showcases the natural sweetness and texture of its seafood components.

PREPARATION TIME: 15 MINUTES
COOKING TIME: 25 MINUTES
TOTAL TIME: 40 MINUTES
DIFFICULTY: EASY
SERVINGS: 1

PROCEDURE:

1. In a large pot, heat the olive oil over medium heat. Add the onions, carrots, and fennel, sautéing until they begin to soften, about 5 minutes.
2. Pour in the diced tomatoes and fish broth. Bring the mixture to a simmer.
3. Add the mixed seafood to the pot, along with the mixed herbs. Simmer gently until the seafood is cooked through, about 10-15 minutes.
4. Season the soup with salt and pepper to taste. Be careful with the salt, as the seafood and broth already contain salt.
5. Serve the soup hot, garnished with additional herbs if desired.

INGREDIENTS:

- 1 cup mixed seafood (e.g., shrimp, scallops, mussels)
- ½ cup diced tomatoes
- 2 cups low-sodium fish broth
- ¼ cup diced onions
- ¼ cup diced carrots
- ¼ cup diced fennel
- 1 teaspoon mixed herbs (e.g., parsley, thyme)
- 1 tablespoon olive oil
- Salt and pepper, to taste

NUTRITIONAL VALUES (APPROXIMATE):

Calories: 300 kcal; **Carbohydrates:** 20 g; **Proteins:** 30 g; **Fats:** 10 g; **Fiber:** 3 g.

Lean Red Meat

1. PEPPERED BEEF TENDERLOIN WITH ARUGULA SALAD

Introduction:

Enjoy a harmonious blend of flavors with this Peppered Beef Tenderloin with Arugula Salad, a dish that pairs the succulence of perfectly cooked beef tenderloin with the peppery bite of arugula, all topped with shavings of Parmesan and a drizzle of balsamic glaze. It's a sophisticated yet simple meal that's perfect for special occasions or a gourmet weeknight dinner.

PREPARATION TIME: 15 MINUTES
COOKING TIME: 25 MINUTES
TOTAL TIME: 40 MINUTES
DIFFICULTY: MEDIUM
SERVINGS: 1

PROCEDURE:

1. Preheat your oven to 400°F (200°C).
2. Season the beef tenderloin generously with crushed black peppercorns and a pinch of salt.
3. Heat a skillet over medium-high heat and add 1 tablespoon of olive oil. Sear the tenderloin on all sides until golden brown, about 2 minutes per side.
4. Transfer the skillet to the preheated oven and roast the tenderloin to your desired doneness, about 10-15 minutes for medium-rare.
5. Remove the tenderloin from the oven and let it rest for 5 minutes before slicing.
6. While the beef is resting, assemble the salad by tossing the arugula with olive oil, balsamic vinegar, and a pinch of salt.
7. Plate the sliced beef tenderloin on a bed of arugula salad. Top with shaved Parmesan cheese and drizzle with a bit more balsamic vinegar if desired.

INGREDIENTS:

- 6 ounces lean beef tenderloin
- 1 tablespoon black peppercorns, crushed
- 2 cups arugula
- 2 tablespoons shaved Parmesan cheese
- 1 tablespoon olive oil, plus extra for drizzling
- 1 tablespoon balsamic vinegar
- Salt, to taste

NUTRITIONAL VALUES (APPROXIMATE):

Calories: 450 kcal; **Carbohydrates:** 3 g; **Proteins:** 40 g; **Fats:** 30 g; **Fiber:** 1 g.

2. LEAN BEEF MEATBALLS IN TOMATO SAUCE ON POLENTA

Introduction:

This Lean Beef Meatballs in Tomato Sauce on Polenta dish offers a comforting, hearty meal without the guilt. Juicy lean beef meatballs simmered in a rich tomato sauce, served atop creamy polenta, and sprinkled with grated Parmesan cheese; this recipe brings classic Italian flavors to your table in a healthier way.

PREPARATION TIME: 20 MINUTES
COOKING TIME: 30 MINUTES
TOTAL TIME: 50 MINUTES
DIFFICULTY: MEDIUM
SERVINGS: 1

INGREDIENTS:

- 4 ounces lean ground beef
- ½ cup canned tomatoes, crushed
- 1 clove garlic, minced
- ½ cup polenta
- 2 tablespoons grated Parmesan cheese
- 1 tablespoon olive oil
- Salt and pepper, to taste
- Fresh herbs (basil or parsley), for garnishing

PROCEDURE:

1. Mix the lean ground beef with salt, pepper, and minced garlic. Form into small meatballs.
2. Heat a pan over medium heat and add the meatballs. Cook until browned on all sides, then remove and set aside.
3. In the same pan, add the crushed tomatoes and bring to a simmer. Return the meatballs to the pan, cover, and let simmer for 20 minutes.
4. Meanwhile, prepare the polenta according to package instructions, seasoning with salt to taste.
5. Serve the meatballs and tomato sauce over a bed of polenta. Sprinkle with grated Parmesan cheese and garnish with fresh herbs.

NUTRITIONAL VALUES (APPROXIMATE):

Calories: 500 kcal; **Carbohydrates:** 45 g; **Proteins:** 30 g; **Fats:** 22 g; **Fiber:** 5 g.

3. FLORENTINE-STYLE BEEF STEAK WITH GRILLED VEGETABLES

Introduction:

Immerse yourself in the heart of Tuscany with this Florentine-style Beef Steak served alongside a medley of grilled vegetables. This dish celebrates the simplicity and quality of its ingredients, featuring a perfectly grilled lean beef steak seasoned with rosemary, accompanied by zucchini, bell peppers, and eggplant. It's a feast that brings the essence of Italian cooking to your table.

PREPARATION TIME: 15 MINUTES
COOKING TIME: 15 MINUTES
TOTAL TIME: 30 MINUTES
DIFFICULTY: EASY
SERVINGS: 1

INGREDIENTS:

- 6 ounces lean beef steak
- ½ zucchini, sliced
- ½ bell pepper, sliced
- ½ eggplant, sliced
- 1 tablespoon olive oil
- 1 teaspoon fresh rosemary, chopped
- Salt and pepper, to taste

PROCEDURE:

1. Preheat your grill to a high heat.
2. Season the beef steak with salt, pepper, and rosemary.
3. Lightly brush the zucchini, bell pepper, and eggplant slices with olive oil and season with salt and pepper.
4. Grill the steak to your desired doneness, about 3-4 minutes per side for medium-rare, depending on thickness.
5. Grill the vegetables until tender and slightly charred, about 2-3 minutes per side.
6. Let the steak rest for a few minutes before slicing.
7. Serve the sliced beef steak with the grilled vegetables on the side.

NUTRITIONAL VALUES (APPROXIMATE):

Calories: 450 kcal; **Carbohydrates:** 15 g; **Proteins:** 40 g; **Fats:** 25 g; **Fiber:** 5 g.

4. LEAN BEEF STEW WITH WINTER VEGETABLES

Introduction:
Warm up with this comforting Lean Beef Stew with Winter Vegetables, a wholesome and hearty dish that combines tender pieces of lean beef with a bounty of winter vegetables, all simmered slowly in a rich, flavorful broth. This stew is a perfect way to enjoy a balanced, satisfying meal on a cold day.

PREPARATION TIME: 20 MINUTES
COOKING TIME: 2 HOURS
TOTAL TIME: 2 HOURS 20 MINUTES
DIFFICULTY: MEDIUM
SERVINGS: 1

INGREDIENTS:

- 6 ounces lean beef, cubed
- ½ cup diced potatoes
- ½ cup diced carrots
- ½ cup diced celery
- ¼ cup diced onions
- 2 cups low-sodium beef broth
- 1 teaspoon fresh thyme
- 1 tablespoon olive oil
- Salt and pepper, to taste

PROCEDURE:

1. Heat the olive oil in a large pot over medium heat. Add the beef cubes and brown on all sides.
2. Add the onions, carrots, celery, and potatoes to the pot. Cook for a few minutes until the vegetables start to soften.
3. Pour in the beef broth and add the thyme. Season with salt and pepper.
4. Bring the stew to a boil, then reduce the heat to low. Cover and simmer for about 2 hours, or until the beef is tender and the vegetables are cooked through.
5. Adjust the seasoning as needed and serve hot.

NUTRITIONAL VALUES (APPROXIMATE):

Calories: 500 kcal; **Carbohydrates:** 30 g; **Proteins:** 40 g; **Fats:** 22 g; **Fiber:** 6 g.

5. SPICY THAI BEEF SALAD

Introduction:
Experience the vibrant flavors of Thailand with this Spicy Thai Beef Salad, a refreshing and zesty dish that combines grilled lean beef strips with crisp lettuce, juicy tomatoes, and crisp cucumbers, all tossed in a spicy lime dressing. It's a perfect balance of heat, sweetness, and acidity, making for an unforgettable meal.

PREPARATION TIME: 20 MINUTES
COOKING TIME: 10 MINUTES
TOTAL TIME: 30 MINUTES
DIFFICULTY: EASY
SERVINGS: 1

INGREDIENTS:

- 6 ounces lean beef strips
- 2 cups lettuce, torn
- ½ cup tomatoes, sliced
- ½ cup cucumbers, sliced
- 1 tablespoon fresh coriander, chopped
- 1 tablespoon fresh mint, chopped
- 1 small chili, sliced
- 2 tablespoons fish sauce
- 1 tablespoon lime juice
- 1 teaspoon sugar
- 1 tablespoon olive oil

PROCEDURE:

1. Heat the olive oil in a pan over medium-high heat. Add the beef strips and cook until just done, about 3-4 minutes. Set aside to cool slightly.
2. In a large bowl, combine the lettuce, tomatoes, cucumbers, coriander, mint, and chili.
3. In a small bowl, whisk together the fish sauce, lime juice, and sugar until the sugar is dissolved.
4. Add the cooked beef strips to the salad. Pour the dressing over the salad and toss well to combine.
5. Serve immediately, enjoying the mix of spicy, tangy, and savory flavors.

NUTRITIONAL VALUES (APPROXIMATE):

Calories: 400 kcal; **Carbohydrates:** 15 g; **Proteins:** 40 g; **Fats:** 20 g; **Fiber:** 3 g.

CHAPTER 14
DESSERTS

1. OAT AND BANANA COOKIES

Introduction:

Satisfy your sweet tooth with these wholesome Oat and Banana Cookies, a simple and nutritious dessert made with just a few ingredients. Combining the natural sweetness of ripe bananas with whole oats and raisins, these cookies are a healthy alternative to traditional sweets, perfect for snacking or breakfast on the go.

PREPARATION TIME: 10 MINUTES
COOKING TIME: 15 MINUTES
TOTAL TIME: 25 MINUTES
DIFFICULTY: EASY
SERVINGS: 12 COOKIES

PROCEDURE:

1. Preheat the oven to 350°F (175°C) and line a baking sheet with parchment paper.
2. In a bowl, combine the mashed bananas, whole oats, raisins, cinnamon, and vanilla extract until well mixed.
3. Drop spoonful of the mixture onto the prepared baking sheet, shaping into cookies.
4. Bake in the preheated oven for 15 minutes, or until the edges are golden brown.
5. Let the cookies cool on the baking sheet for a few minutes before transferring to a wire rack to cool completely.

INGREDIENTS:

- 2 ripe bananas, mashed
- 1 cup whole oats
- ½ cup raisins
- ½ teaspoon cinnamon
- 1 teaspoon vanilla extract

NUTRITIONAL VALUES (APPROXIMATE, PER COOKIE):

Calories: 70 kcal; **Carbohydrates:** 15 g; **Proteins:** 2 g; **Fats:** 0.5 g; **Fiber:** 2 g.

2. AVOCADO AND CACAO MOUSSE

Introduction:

Indulge in the rich and creamy texture of Avocado and Cacao Mousse, a decadent yet healthy dessert that combines the nutritional benefits of avocado with the intense flavor of cocoa powder. Sweetened naturally with maple syrup and enhanced with a hint of vanilla, this mousse is a guilt-free treat that chocolate lovers will adore.

PREPARATION TIME: 10 MINUTES
CHILLING TIME: 1 HOUR
TOTAL TIME: 1 HOUR 10 MINUTES
DIFFICULTY: EASY
SERVINGS: 2

PROCEDURE:

1. Scoop the flesh of the avocado into a blender.
2. Add the cocoa powder, maple syrup, vanilla extract, and sea salt to the blender.
3. Blend until smooth and creamy, scraping down the sides as needed.
4. Divide the mousse into serving dishes and chill in the refrigerator for at least 1 hour before serving.

INGREDIENTS:

- 1 ripe avocado
- ¼ cup cocoa powder
- 3 tablespoons maple syrup
- ½ teaspoon vanilla extract
- A pinch of sea salt

NUTRITIONAL VALUES (APPROXIMATE, PER SERVING):

Calories: 250 kcal; **Carbohydrates:** 35 g; **Proteins:** 4 g; **Fats:** 14 g; **Fiber:** 8 g.

3. DATE AND NUT BARS

Introduction:
Power up with these Date and Nut Bars, a dense and chewy snack packed with the natural sweetness of dates and the crunch of mixed nuts. Enhanced with chia seeds and cocoa powder for an extra nutritional boost, these bars are perfect for a quick energy lift or a satisfying dessert.

PREPARATION TIME: 15 MINUTES
SETTING TIME: 2 HOURS
TOTAL TIME: 2 HOURS 15 MINUTES
DIFFICULTY: EASY
SERVINGS: 8 BARS

INGREDIENTS:
- 1 cup pitted dates
- ½ cup mixed nuts (such as almonds, walnuts, and pecans)
- 2 tablespoons chia seeds
- 2 tablespoons cocoa powder
- ¼ cup dried coconut

PROCEDURE:
1. Line an 8-inch square baking pan with parchment paper.
2. In a food processor, blend the dates, nuts, chia seeds, and cocoa powder until the mixture forms a sticky dough.
3. Press the mixture firmly into the prepared pan, creating an even layer.
4. Sprinkle the dried coconut over the top and press lightly to adhere.
5. Chill in the refrigerator for at least 2 hours, or until firm.
6. Cut into bars and serve. Store any leftovers in an airtight container in the refrigerator.

NUTRITIONAL VALUES (APPROXIMATE, PER BAR):
Calories: 180 kcal; **Carbohydrates:** 20 g; **Proteins:** 4 g; **Fats:** 10 g; **Fiber:** 4 g.

4. GREEK YOGURT AND FRESH FRUIT TART

Introduction:
Embrace the delight of a Greek Yogurt and Fresh Fruit Tart, where a wholesome whole wheat cookie crust cradles creamy low-fat Greek yogurt, sweetened with honey and topped with a vibrant array of fresh fruits. This dessert elegantly combines health with taste, making it a perfect choice for a refreshing treat or a special occasion.

PREPARATION TIME: 20 MINUTES
COOKING TIME: 10 MINUTES (FOR THE BASE)
CHILLING TIME: 2 HOURS
TOTAL TIME: 2 HOURS 30 MINUTES
DIFFICULTY: MEDIUM
SERVINGS: 8

INGREDIENTS FOR THE BASE:
- 1 cup whole wheat flour
- ¼ cup coconut oil, melted
- 2 tablespoons honey
- 1 teaspoon vanilla extract

INGREDIENTS FOR THE FILLING:
- 2 cups low-fat Greek yogurt
- 2 tablespoons honey
- 1 teaspoon vanilla extract

TOPPING:
- Assorted fresh fruit (such as strawberries, kiwi, blueberries, and raspberries)

PROCEDURE:
1. Preheat the oven to 350°F (175°C). Mix the whole wheat flour, melted coconut oil, honey, and vanilla extract in a bowl until a dough forms.
2. Press the dough into a tart pan, evenly covering the bottom and sides.
3. Bake the crust for 10 minutes, or until lightly golden. Allow to cool completely.
4. In a separate bowl, mix the Greek yogurt with honey and vanilla extract until smooth.
5. Pour the yogurt mixture into the cooled crust and spread evenly.
6. Arrange the fresh fruit on top of the yogurt in a decorative pattern.
7. Chill the tart in the refrigerator for at least 2 hours before serving.

NUTRITIONAL VALUES (APPROXIMATE, PER SERVING):
Calories: 200 kcal; **Carbohydrates:** 25 g; **Proteins:** 10 g; **Fats:** 8 g; **Fiber:** 3 g.

5. HOMEMADE BANANA ICE CREAM

Introduction:
Savor the natural sweetness and creamy texture of Homemade Banana Ice Cream, a delightful dessert made with frozen ripe bananas and a hint of vanilla. This simple, dairy-free ice cream is enriched with almond milk and dark chocolate chips for an extra layer of flavor and indulgence, making it a guilt-free treat for any occasion.

PREPARATION TIME: 10 MINUTES (PLUS FREEZING TIME)
TOTAL TIME: 10 MINUTES (PLUS FREEZING TIME)
DIFFICULTY: EASY
SERVINGS: 2

PROCEDURE:
1. Place the frozen banana slices, vanilla extract, and almond milk in a blender or food processor.
2. Blend until smooth and creamy, scraping down the sides as necessary.
3. Stir in the dark chocolate chips.
4. Serve immediately for a soft-serve texture, or transfer to a container and freeze until firm for a more traditional ice cream consistency.

INGREDIENTS:
*   3 ripe bananas, sliced and frozen
*   ½ teaspoon vanilla extract
*   ¼ cup almond milk
*   ¼ cup dark chocolate chips

NUTRITIONAL VALUES (APPROXIMATE, PER SERVING):
Calories: 280 kcal; **Carbohydrates:** 50 g; **Proteins:** 3 g; **Fats:** 8 g; **Fiber:** 5 g.

6. LIGHT OAT AND BLUEBERRY PANCAKES

Introduction:
Enjoy a healthier twist on a breakfast favorite with Light Oat and Blueberry Pancakes. Made with whole oats and almond milk, and bursting with fresh blueberries, these pancakes offer a nutritious start to your day or a delightful dessert option. Drizzled with pure maple syrup, they're sure to satisfy your pancake cravings in a lighter way.

PREPARATION TIME: 10 MINUTES
COOKING TIME: 10 MINUTES
TOTAL TIME: 20 MINUTES
DIFFICULTY: EASY
SERVINGS: 4 PANCAKES

PROCEDURE:
1. In a bowl, mix the oat flour, almond milk, and eggs until well combined.
2. Gently fold in the fresh blueberries.
3. Heat a non-stick skillet over medium heat and lightly coat with cooking spray or oil.
4. Pour ¼ of the batter into the skillet for each pancake. Cook until bubbles form on the surface, then flip and cook until golden brown on the other side.
5. Serve the pancakes warm, drizzled with maple syrup.

INGREDIENTS:
*   1 cup whole oats, ground into flour
*   1 cup almond milk
*   2 eggs
*   1 cup fresh blueberries
*   2 tablespoons pure maple syrup
*   Cooking spray or a small amount of oil for the pan

NUTRITIONAL VALUES (APPROXIMATE, PER SERVING/PANCAKE):
Calories: 150 kcal; **Carbohydrates:** 22 g; **Proteins:** 6 g; **Fats:** 4 g; **Fiber:** 3 g.

7. RASPBERRY SORBET

Introduction:

Experience the pure, refreshing taste of Raspberry Sorbet, a light and fruity dessert perfect for cooling down on a warm day. Made with frozen raspberries blended to perfection with orange juice and a touch of honey for sweetness, this sorbet is a simple pleasure that's sure to delight your palate.

PREPARATION TIME: 10 MINUTES (PLUS FREEZING TIME)
TOTAL TIME: 10 MINUTES (PLUS FREEZING TIME)
DIFFICULTY: EASY
SERVINGS: 4

INGREDIENTS:

- 2 cups frozen raspberries
- ½ cup orange juice
- 2 tablespoons honey
- ½ cup water

PROCEDURE:

1. In a blender, combine the frozen raspberries, orange juice, honey, and water. Blend until smooth.
2. Taste and adjust sweetness, if necessary, by adding a little more honey.
3. Pour the mixture into a shallow dish and freeze until solid, about 2-3 hours.
4. Before serving, let the sorbet sit at room temperature for a few minutes to soften slightly. Then, scoop into bowls or glasses.

NUTRITIONAL VALUES (APPROXIMATE, PER SERVING):

Calories: 100 kcal; **Carbohydrates:** 25 g; **Proteins:** 1 g; **Fats:** 0 g; **Fiber:** 4 g.

8. LIGHT CARROT CUPCAKES

Introduction:

Savor the classic taste of carrot cake in a healthier form with these Light Carrot Cupcakes. Made with whole wheat flour, grated carrots, and apples for natural sweetness, these cupcakes are a nutritious alternative to traditional desserts. Topped with a light Greek yogurt frosting, they're perfect for satisfying your sweet tooth without the guilt.

PREPARATION TIME: 20 MINUTES
COOKING TIME: 20 MINUTES
TOTAL TIME: 40 MINUTES
DIFFICULTY: MEDIUM
SERVINGS: 12 CUPCAKES

INGREDIENTS FOR THE CUPCAKES:

- 1 cup whole wheat flour
- 1 ½ cups grated carrots
- ½ cup grated apples
- 2 eggs
- ¼ cup coconut oil, melted
- ½ cup honey
- 1 teaspoon cinnamon
- ½ teaspoon nutmeg
- 1 teaspoon baking powder
- ½ teaspoon baking soda

INGREDIENTS FOR THE FROSTING:

- 1 cup low-fat Greek yogurt
- 2 tablespoons honey
- ½ teaspoon vanilla extract

PROCEDURE:

1. Preheat the oven to 350°F (175°C) and line a muffin tin with cupcake liners.
2. In a large bowl, mix together the whole wheat flour, cinnamon, nutmeg, baking powder, and baking soda.
3. In a separate bowl, whisk the eggs with melted coconut oil and honey until well combined. Stir in the grated carrots and apples.
4. Gradually add the wet ingredients to the dry ingredients, stirring until just combined.
5. Divide the batter evenly among the cupcake liners and bake for 20 minutes, or until a toothpick inserted into the center comes out clean.
6. While the cupcakes are baking, prepare the frosting by mixing the Greek yogurt, honey, and vanilla extract until smooth. Refrigerate until ready to use.
7. Allow the cupcakes to cool completely before frosting them with the Greek yogurt mixture.
8. Serve and enjoy these light and moist cupcakes, each bite filled with the flavors of carrot, apple, and spices.

NUTRITIONAL VALUES (APPROXIMATE, PER CUPCAKE WITH FROSTING):

Calories: 180 kcal; **Carbohydrates:** 27 g; **Proteins:** 5 g; **Fats:** 6 g; **Fiber:** 3 g.

28-DAY MEAL PLAN

DAY	BREAKFAST	SNACK	LUNCH	AFTERNOON SNACK	DINNER
1	Oat and Banana Muffins	Greek Yogurt with Honey and Almonds	Mediterranean Quinoa Salad	Carrot Sticks and Hummus	Grilled Chicken Breast with Avocado Salsa
2	Berry and Seed Smoothie Bowl	Fresh Fruit Salad with Mint	Whole Wheat Spring Pasta	Steamed Edamame with Sea Salt	Baked Salmon with Avocado Sauce
3	Scrambled Eggs with Spinach and Whole Grain Toast	Cottage Cheese with Pineapple	Thai Beef Salad	Homemade Energy Bars	Vegetarian Tacos with Black Beans
4	Chia Seed Pudding with Coconut Milk	Celery Boats with Peanut Butter and Raisins	Greek Chickpea Salad	Spiced Toasted Nuts	Lean Beef Chili with Beans
5	Whole Blueberry Muffins	Avocado and Tomato Crostini	Farro with Roasted Vegetables	Baked Kale Chips	Shrimp Tacos with Spicy Coleslaw
6	Banana and Oat Pancakes	Sliced Apples with Almond Butter	Barley with Cherry Tomatoes and Arugula	Cucumber and Lemon Infused Water (with a side of nuts)	Rosemary Beef Tenderloin with Steamed Vegetables
7	Protein Coffee Smoothie	Greek Yogurt and Fresh Berries	Bulgur, Cucumber, and Mint Salad	Quinoa and Black Bean Burgers (miniature version)	Whole Wheat Squid Ink Spaghetti with Seafood
8	Avocado Toast on Whole Grain Bread	Mixed Nuts and Dried Fruit	Lentil Soup with Whole Wheat Roll	Greek Yogurt with Blueberries	Grilled Vegetable and Quinoa Salad
9	Smoothie with Spinach, Banana, and Almond Butter	Carrot and Cucumber Sticks with Hummus	Chicken Caesar Wrap with Light Dressing	Apple Slices with Peanut Butter	Baked Cod with Roasted Sweet Potatoes and Green Beans

DAY	BREAKFAST	SNACK	LUNCH	AFTERNOON SNACK	DINNER
10	Cottage Cheese with Pineapple Chunks	A Handful of Almonds	Turkey and Avocado Salad	Bell Pepper Strips with Guacamole	Stir-Fried Tofu with Broccoli and Brown Rice
11	Omelet with Spinach, Tomatoes, and Feta Cheese	A Pear	Quinoa Salad with Cucumber, Kalamata Olives, and Feta	Whole Grain Crackers with Cheese	Lemon Herb Salmon with Asparagus and Quinoa
12	Banana and Walnut Oatmeal	A Peach	Chickpea and Roasted Vegetable Wrap	Edamame with Sea Salt	Beef Stir-Fry with Mixed Vegetables and Brown Rice
13	Greek Yogurt Parfait with Mixed Berries and Granola	Raw Veggies with Ranch Dip	Sardine Salad on Whole Grain Toast	Cottage Cheese with Sliced Strawberries	Spaghetti Squash with Marinara Sauce and Meatballs
14	Scrambled Eggs with Mushrooms and Onions	A Banana	Tuna Salad Stuffed Avocado	Dark Chocolate Square and Almonds	Grilled Chicken with Sweet Potato Fries and Steamed Broccoli
15	Whole Grain Pancakes with Fresh Berries	Rice Cakes with Almond Butter	Spinach and Goat Cheese Stuffed Chicken Breast with Quinoa	Fresh Pineapple Chunks	Vegetarian Chili
16	Scrambled Tofu with Spinach and Tomatoes	Greek Yogurt with Honey and Slivered Almonds	Quinoa and Roasted Vegetable Salad with Lemon-Tahini Dressing	Cucumber Slices with Hummus	Pan-Seared Tilapia with Steamed Broccoli and Wild Rice
17	Chia Seed Pudding with Mango and Coconut Flakes	A Handful of Walnuts	Turkey, Avocado, and Bacon Wrap	Baby Carrots and Bell Pepper Strips	Eggplant Parmesan
18	Berry Smoothie with Spinach, Greek Yogurt, and Flaxseeds	Hard-Boiled Eggs	Soba Noodle Salad with Peanut Sauce	Apple with Peanut Butter	Grilled Shrimp Skewers with Mixed Greens Salad
19	Oatmeal with Sliced Banana and Cinnamon	Cottage Cheese with Sliced Peaches	Mediterranean Lentil Salad	Mixed Berry Fruit Salad	Baked Chicken Thighs with Brussels Sprouts and Sweet Potatoes

DAY	BREAKFAST	SNACK	LUNCH	AFTERNOON SNACK	DINNER
20	Toasted Whole Grain Bread with Avocado and Tomato Slices	A Handful of Pumpkin Seeds	Grilled Portobello Mushroom Burgers	Sliced Pear with Cheese	Salmon Caesar Salad
21	Green Detox Smoothie	A Small Bowl of Mixed Nuts	Chicken and Avocado Salad with Lime-Cilantro Dressing	Sliced Cucumbers with Tzatziki Sauce	Zucchini Noodles with Pesto and Cherry Tomatoes
22	Avocado and Egg Breakfast Pizza	Kiwi and Strawberry Slices	Spicy Lentil Soup with Whole Grain Bread	Low-fat Cheese Sticks	Grilled Lamb Chops with Mint Yogurt Sauce and Couscous Salad
23	Quinoa Porridge with Apple and Cinnamon	Roasted Chickpeas	Rainbow Vegetable Sushi Rolls with Brown Rice	Mixed Berries with a Dollop of Greek Yogurt	Stuffed Bell Peppers with Ground Turkey and Quinoa
24	Nut Butter and Banana Sandwich on Whole Grain Bread	A Handful of Dried Apricots	Cold Pasta Salad with Cherry Tomatoes, Mozzarella, and Basil	Vegetable Sticks with Baba Ganoush	Cod en Papillote with Lemon, Asparagus, and Cherry Tomatoes
25	Yogurt Parfait with Granola and Mango	Whole Grain Crackers with Hummus	Kale, Avocado, and Chickpea Salad with Lemon Vinaigrette	Peach Slices	Beef and Broccoli Stir-Fry over Brown Rice
26	Spinach and Feta Omelette	A Small Bowl of Olives	Tuna Salad Stuffed Avocados	Dark Chocolate and Almond Butter Bites	Vegetarian Black Bean Enchiladas
27	Blueberry and Almond Milk Smoothie	A Small Bag of Popcorn (air-popped)	Chicken Gyro Salad with Tzatziki Sauce	Carrot and Cucumber Sticks with Guacamole	Spaghetti with Clams and Zucchini in White Wine Sauce
28	Breakfast Burrito with Scrambled Eggs, Black Beans, and Salsa	A Pear	Quiche with Spinach and Mushrooms	Greek Yogurt with Honey and Walnuts	Moroccan Tagine with Chickpeas and Vegetables

SHOPPING LIST

Creating a shopping list based on the meal plan requires organizing ingredients by week to ensure freshness, especially for perishables, and efficiency in shopping. Here's an example shopping list for the first week, categorized by food type to make your supermarket trips more streamlined. Adjust quantities based on your household size and the specific days/meals you plan to prepare.

Week 1 Shopping List:

Fruits and Vegetables:
- Bananas
- Mixed berries (strawberries, blueberries, raspberries)
- Fresh pineapples
- Apples
- Avocados
- Lemons and limes
- Cherry tomatoes
- Cucumbers
- Red and green bell peppers
- Red onions
- Spinach
- Arugula
- Broccoli
- Sweet potatoes
- Asparagus
- Zucchini
- Carrots
- Garlic
- Fresh cilantro and mint
- Fresh parsley

Proteins:
- Greek yogurt (low-fat)
- Eggs
- Lean chicken breasts
- Fresh tuna
- Salmon fillets
- Lean beef (for steak and ground)
- Turkey breast slices
- Mixed seafood (for spaghetti)
- Sardines
- Black beans
- Chickpeas
- Lentils

Dairy and Eggs:
- Low-fat feta cheese
- Parmesan cheese
- Low-fat mozzarella cheese
- Cottage cheese

Grains and Bakery:
- Whole oats
- Whole wheat pasta
- Quinoa
- Farro
- Barley
- Bulgur
- Whole wheat tortillas
- Whole wheat bread
- Whole grain crackers

Pantry Staples:
- Olive oil
- Balsamic vinegar
- Low-sodium soy sauce
- Whole wheat breadcrumbs
- Rice cakes
- Almond butter
- Peanut butter
- Honey
- Mixed nuts and dried fruit
- Seeds (chia, flaxseed, sesame)
- Spices (cumin, chili powder, smoked paprika, cinnamon)
- Whole wheat squid ink spaghetti
- Low-sodium vegetable broth
- Tomato sauce
- Coconut milk
- Brown rice
- Couscous

Beverages:
- Almond milk
- Coconut water

Snacks and Others:
- Dark chocolate
- Air-popped popcorn

Week 2 Shopping List:

Fruits and Vegetables:

- Kiwis
- Strawberries
- Pineapples
- Mangoes
- Peaches
- Mixed lettuce leaves
- Baby spinach
- Red cabbage
- Edamame
- Mixed fresh berries for snacks and salads
- Additional avocados
- Cherry tomatoes (for salads and toppings)
- More cucumbers
- Additional carrots and celery for snacking
- Fresh ginger

Proteins:

- Fresh or frozen shrimp
- Fresh squid (for Whole Wheat Squid Ink Spaghetti with Seafood)
- Lean beef (for different variations like chili or salads)
- Canned sardines (if not leftover from week 1)
- Canned or dried lentils and black beans (if needing replenishment)

Dairy and Eggs:

- Continue with Greek yogurt, low-fat cheeses, and eggs, replenishing as needed.

Grains and Bakery:

- Restock whole wheat pasta and bread as needed.
- Additional whole grain tortillas for wraps and tacos.
- More quinoa and bulgur if running low.

Pantry Staples:

- Olive oil and balsamic vinegar (replenish if low).
- A variety of spices (add any specific ones needed for new recipes).
- More honey or maple syrup for sweetening dishes and dressings.
- Soy sauce and sesame oil (for Asian-inspired dishes).
- Whole wheat breadcrumbs (if needed).
- Coconut or almond milk.

Snacks and Others:

- Nuts and seeds for snacks and salad toppings.
- Whole grain crackers.
- Hummus and guacamole (or avocados to make fresh).

Protein and Seafood:

- A variety of seafood for the Whole Wheat Squid Ink Spaghetti with Seafood.
- Additional lean meats or plant-based proteins based on your preferences and the week's recipes.

Frozen Goods:

- Frozen berries (for smoothies and yogurt toppings).
- Additional frozen vegetables if desired for quick sides.

Notes:

- Review recipes for specific quantities to ensure you have enough, especially for perishable items like fruits and vegetables.
- Plan for leftovers to reduce waste and save on cooking time. Many dinners can serve as the next day's lunch.
- Adjust based on preferences: If there are meals you particularly enjoyed from Week 1, consider repeating them in Week 2 and simply adjust your shopping list accordingly.

Week 3 Shopping List:

Fruits and Vegetables:
- Mangoes
- Apples
- Kiwis
- Strawberries
- Pineapple
- Cucumbers
- Carrots
- Red cabbage
- Mixed lettuce leaves
- Bell peppers (various colors)
- Broccoli
- Zucchini
- Cherry tomatoes
- Asparagus
- Lemons and limes
- Fresh cilantro
- Fresh mint
- Avocados
- Peaches

Proteins:
- Tofu (firm or extra-firm)
- Fresh tuna steaks
- Shrimp (peeled and deveined)
- Lamb chops
- Mixed seafood (for paella or stir-fry)

Dairy and Eggs:
- Greek yogurt (low-fat)
- Feta cheese (low-fat)
- Parmesan cheese
- Cottage cheese
- Eggs

Grains and Bakery:
- Whole grain bread
- Brown rice
- Soba noodles
- Whole wheat tortillas
- Quinoa
- Couscous

Pantry Staples:
- Olive oil
- Sesame oil
- Low-sodium soy sauce
- Peanut butter
- Honey
- Balsamic vinegar
- Rice vinegar
- Sesame seeds
- Chickpeas
- Lentils
- Black beans
- Quinoa
- Dried apricots
- Walnuts
- Almonds
- Popcorn kernels (for air-popping)
- Whole grain crackers

Protein Powders and Supplements:
- Protein powder (if desired for smoothies or baking)

Herbs, Spices, and Condiments:
- Fresh rosemary
- Chili flakes
- Paprika
- Cumin
- Garlic powder
- Turmeric
- Curry powder
- Fish sauce
- Tahini

Beverages:
- Almond milk
- Coconut water

Snacks and Others:
- Dark chocolate
- Almond butter
- Pumpkin seeds
- Dried coconut flakes

Notes for Week 3:
- This list includes ingredients for creating dishes with vibrant flavors, such as Thai Beef Salad, Spicy Lentil Soup, and Grilled Lamb Chops with Mint Yogurt Sauce.
- Fresh herbs and spices play a significant role in this week's meals, enhancing flavors without adding extra calories.
- Review your pantry for staples before shopping to avoid purchasing duplicates.
- Plan for leftovers by buying slightly more of versatile ingredients like brown rice, quinoa, and mixed vegetables, which can be used in multiple meals throughout the week.

Week 4 Shopping List:

Fruits and Vegetables:

- Mangoes
- Peaches
- Kiwis
- Pears
- Oranges
- Mixed berries for snacks and garnishes
- Avocados (for salads and spreads)
- Mixed lettuce (for salads)
- Kale
- Rainbow vegetables (for sushi rolls)
- Cabbage (for slaw and salads)
- Fresh ginger
- Cilantro and parsley (for garnishing and flavors)
- Cherry tomatoes
- Bell peppers (various colors)
- Cucumbers
- Zucchini (for noodles and sides)
- Eggplants
- Brussels sprouts

Proteins:

- Tofu (for stir-fry and scrambles)
- Chickpeas (for salads and snacks)
- Lentils (for soups and salads)
- Lean beef (for tartare and stir-fry)
- Mixed seafood (for paella and spaghetti)
- Eggs (for breakfast dishes and baking)

Dairy and Eggs:

- Greek yogurt (for breakfast and snacks)
- Low-fat cheese (for snacking and salads)
- Parmesan cheese (for garnishing)

Grains and Bakery:

- Brown rice (for sushi and sides)
- Soba noodles
- Whole grain or whole wheat bread (for bruschetta and sandwiches)
- Whole wheat tortillas (for wraps)
- Quinoa (for salads and sides)
- Whole wheat spaghetti

Pantry Staples:

- Olive oil and extra virgin olive oil
- Vinegars (balsamic, apple cider, red wine)
- Low-sodium soy sauce and fish sauce
- Sesame oil and sesame seeds (for salads and sushi)
- Nuts (almonds, walnuts, cashews for snacks and garnishes)
- Coconut milk (for curries and soups)
- Spices (cumin, chili powder, turmeric, smoked paprika, rosemary)
- Whole grain crackers
- Popcorn kernels (for air-popping)
- Honey and maple syrup (for sweetening)
- Peanut butter and almond butter

Snacks and Others:

- Dark chocolate (for a healthy treat)
- Dried fruits (for snacking and salads)
- Almond milk (for smoothies and breakfast)

Beverages:

- Herbal teas (for hydration and variety)

FAQS REGARDING THE 28-DAY MEAL PLAN

1. Is this meal plan suitable for weight loss? Yes, this meal plan can be suitable for weight loss as it emphasizes whole foods, lean proteins, and a balance of nutrients. Portion control and adjusting calorie intake based on individual needs are essential for weight loss.

2. Can I follow this plan if I have dietary restrictions? Absolutely. This plan is designed to be flexible. For dietary restrictions such as gluten intolerance, dairy sensitivity, or vegetarian preferences, substitute appropriate alternatives for any ingredients that don't fit your dietary needs.

3. How can I make sure I'm getting enough protein on this plan? The plan includes a variety of protein sources, including lean meats, fish, dairy, and plant-based proteins like beans and lentils. Ensuring you include these items in your daily meals will help meet protein needs.

4. What if I don't have time to prepare meals from scratch every day? Consider meal prepping in advance. Many ingredients can be prepared in bulk and stored in the fridge or freezer. Also, look for simpler recipes or healthy pre-made options for particularly busy days.

5. Are snacks necessary? Snacks are included to help manage hunger and provide energy throughout the day. If you're not hungry or prefer fewer meals, it's okay to skip them. Listen to your body's hunger cues.

6. Can I swap meals from one day to another? Yes, you can swap meals as you see fit. The plan provides a structure, but flexibility is key to sticking with any long-term dietary changes. Just ensure each day remains balanced.

7. How can I adjust the meal plan for my caloric needs? Calculate your daily caloric needs based on factors like age, gender, weight, and activity level. Adjust portion sizes or add/remove snacks to align the meal plan with your caloric requirements.

8. What should I do if I'm experiencing cravings? Cravings are normal. Allow yourself occasional treats but try to find healthier alternatives that satisfy your craving without derailing your dietary goals. Hydration and fiber-rich snacks can also help manage cravings.

9. How can I ensure I stay hydrated? Drink plenty of water throughout the day, aiming for at least 8 glasses. You can also include herbal teas and infused waters. Listen to your thirst cues and increase intake during hot weather or exercise.

10. Is it expensive to follow this meal plan? While some ingredients may seem costly upfront, buying in bulk, choosing seasonal produce, and utilizing leftovers can help manage expenses. Planning and preparation reduce the likelihood of purchasing expensive convenience foods, balancing overall costs. This meal plan is designed to be adaptable, providing a foundation for healthy eating while allowing for the flexibility needed to fit it into a wide range of lifestyles and dietary needs.

INDEX OF INGREDIENTS

Made in the USA
Monee, IL
19 December 2024

74629954R00044